PREVAIL PRAYERS AND PREVAILING FAITH

Best prayer book! Discover the importance of fervent prayers and the power of prayer—Christian deliverance prayers + 300 other prayers that help in life

Kenneth Omeje

KINGDOM BOOKS

Copyright © Kenneth Omeje, 2025

Published by Kingdom Books, an imprint of *CreativeJuicesBooks, Singapore (www.creativejuicesbooks.com)*

All rights reserved. Except for brief quotations in printed reviews, no part of this book may be reproduced, stored in a retrieval system, or transmitted in any form or by any means—electronic, mechanical, digital, photocopy, recording, or any other—without prior permission in writing from the publisher.

All Scripture quotations, unless otherwise indicated, are taken from the *Holy Bible: New King James Version*®. Copyright © 1982 by Thomas Nelson. Used by permission. All rights reserved.

Scripture quotations marked *KJV* are taken from the *Holy Bible: King James Version*.

Scripture quotations marked *AMP* are taken from the *Amplified® Bible*, copyright © 1954, 1958, 1962, 1964, 1965, 1987 by The Lockman Foundation. Used by permission.

Scripture quotations marked *RSV* are taken from the *Revised Standard Version of the Bible*, copyright © 1946, 1952, and 1971 National Council of the Churches of Christ in the United States of America. Used by permission. All rights reserved worldwide.

Scripture quotations marked *NRSVA* are taken from the *New Revised Standard Version: Anglicised Edition*, copyright © 1989, 1995 National Council of the Churches of Christ in the United States of America. Used by permission. All rights reserved worldwide.

Scripture quotations marked *NIV* are taken from the *Holy Bible: New International Version* ®. Copyright © 1973, 1978, 1984 International Bible Society. Used by permission of Zondervan Bible Publishers. All rights reserved.

Scripture quotations marked *TLB* are taken from *The Living Bible*. Copyright © 1971. Used by permission of Tyndale House Publishers, Inc. All rights reserved.

Scripture quotations marked *NLT* are taken from the *Holy Bible, New Living Translation*, copyright © 1996, 2004, 2015 by Tyndale House Foundation. Used by permission of Tyndale House Publishers, Inc., Illinois 60188. All rights reserved.

ISBN 978-981-94-1555-7

Abbreviations Used in This Book

IJN — In Jesus' Name
AKN — Acne Keloidalis Nuchae
NHS — National Health Service

Contents

Acknowledgments		*iv*
Introduction: The Purpose of This Book		*v*

PART 1: PREVAILING PRAYERS

1	The Pervading Power of Prayer	*13*
2	Prayers That Will Not Receive Answers from God	*26*
3	Prayers That Will Receive Answers from God	*34*
	Praying in Accordance with God's Will: Examples	*46*
4	Our Lord's Prayer and Beyond	*61*
	Major Types of Prayers	*62*
	Individual Prayer versus Corporate Prayer and God's Responsiveness	*74*

PART 2: PREVAILING IN THE BATTLES OF LIFE BY YOUR OWN FAITH

5	Understanding and Fighting the Battles of Life	*81*
6	Living by Your Own Faith — Personal Faith	*103*
	Key Points to Explain Personal Faith	*106*
7	Varying Measures of Faith	*119*
8	Heroes in the Bible and Their Works of Personal Faith	*129*

PART 3: ADDITIONAL PRAYERS FOR DIVERSE PURPOSES AND NEEDS   *137*

Endnotes	*163*
Bibliography	*165*
Index	*166*
About the Author	*168*

Acknowledgments

I wish to extend my deepest appreciation to my wife Ngozi and children, Rejoicing, Chibia and Ifediche, for their extraordinary endurance and understanding over the long hours I spent at home writing this book.
Ursula Chok Soo Lang, the Kingdom Books publisher at CreativeJuicesBooks in Singapore, and her team deserve a special commendation for their excellent copyediting, manuscript preparation and professionalism.
I am also grateful to the leaders and members of Crown of Christ Gospel Church in Bradford for their prayers and solidarity.
Above all, I am grateful to the Holy Spirit for the opportunity and illumination to write this book.

Introduction

The Purpose of This Book

This book has been conceived to shine light on the power of prayer and how Christians can, through different types of prayers, deploy their personal faith to prevail over the troubles of life. For most people, rich or poor, life on earth is full of troubling challenges. Neither the godly nor the ungodly are immune from the storms of life—a reality that has exercised the minds of theologians and philosophers in all generations.

Why are countless people in our world dying from poverty, sickness and disease, when many of these deaths are avoidable? Why is there so much violent crime in many towns and cities around the world? Why do we have wars that so viciously and senselessly kill so many innocent people, including children, for reasons they know nothing about? Why is there so much persecution, around the world, of many well-meaning people on account of their ethnic origin, skin colour, or religion?

Why is it that too many "bad people", whose atrocities devastate our world (think of rapists, vicious terrorists, despots, murderers, warmongers, grand looters of public treasuries, and violent burglars), live long lives—while too many of the much-needed "good people", who work so hard to make the world a better place, die prematurely in car crashes, plane crashes, or as victims of those very same "bad people"? Why do natural disasters like earthquakes, hurricanes, cyclones and floods claim so many lives each year, including the lives of too many "good and innocent people"? I do not know if any of my readers have answers to these mind-boggling questions.

Why is it that some of the world's most prayerful countries, with large Christian populations, are apparently among the worst governed and most distressing places to live on earth? These are some of the countries with the world's worst performance records in terms of human development, citizens' safety, and people's overall satisfaction with their quality of life and how their country is governed.[1]

Why is life seemingly more comfortable in some of the least evangelized, non-Christian countries, where other gods are worshipped? Where is the good God of the Bible, the sovereign God of the universe, in all these unexplainable odds of life? The mystery, of why bad things happen to some "good people" whilst many "evil people" receive goodness from God, is not new. Various wise men and prophets of old in the Bible have pondered over this mystery. Does God delight in human suffering, misery and preventable deaths? Why is God sometimes silent when the wicked oppress, persecute, and even kill the righteous? Is God responsible for all these devastating problems in our world? With His incredible sovereign power, why can't God intervene to stop the mess and establish order, justice, security and good governance in every part of the world?

I cannot claim to have answers to most of these existential concerns and philosophical questions. But the revealed word of the Creator of the universe—the Holy Scriptures—has the answers, which I am not offering to comprehensively explain in this book. However, it suffices to say that prayer and faith are powerful keys that God has given us (though not the only keys) to deploy in mitigating or ending human suffering and everything else that is undesirable in any part of the world, especially in our homes or assigned areas of jurisdiction:

> **Is anyone among you suffering? Let him pray.** Is any cheerful? Let him sing praise… Therefore confess your sins to one another, and pray for one another, that you may be healed. **The prayer of a righteous man has great power in its effects.** Elijah was a man of like nature with ourselves and he prayed fervently that it might not rain, and for three years and six months it did not rain on the earth. Then he prayed again and the heaven gave rain, and the earth brought forth its fruit.
>
> *James 5:13, 16-18, RSV*

If, under the comparatively inferior old covenant, Elijah could single-handedly handle the elements of nature, to suspend rain on earth and later release it after three and a half years—all by his prayers—then there is so much that our altruistic prayers could accomplish today under the new covenant, which is a superior and perfect covenant.

The Purpose of This Book

The challenge is that, too often, our prayers are self-centred petitions about our personal and family needs. Elijah's prayers were about the spiritual and governance conditions of the nation of Israel. He prayed fervently and made declarations by faith over Israel, and his words prevailed. There are prevailing prayers, and there is prevailing faith.

It is by prayer, especially the prayers of the righteous, that God is invited from heaven to intervene on earth. But (you may well be asking) wouldn't God in His goodness intervene to end the sufferings and troubles of many innocent people on earth—even if nobody prayerfully invites Him? The answer from the Bible is apparently "no". God has revealed His divine nature, His will and His ways to us in the Bible, including His covenant principles and promises, as well as the conditions for His engagement and operation on earth.

The earth realm is a place that God temporarily leased to mankind when He created the first humans, Adam and Eve. But when Adam and Eve sinned by rebelling against God in the Garden of Eden and obeying Satan, they lost their lease and dominion mandate —thereby surrendering the earth to Satan and his cohort of wicked, contrary spirits, whose principal agenda on earth (as the Bible reveals) is to kill, to steal, and to destroy God's creation, plans and good works.

That is why, in the Bible, Satan is severally described as "the god of this world", "the deceiver of the whole world", "the prince of the power of the air", "the ruler of darkness" and "Beelzebub", or "the ruler of demons," implying that he presides over an organized system of spiritual power by which he strives to control and rule over the world. We can extrapolate from the Bible that Satan and all the fallen angels who rebelled with him against God in heaven were already cast down to the earth before God created the first humans, Adam and Eve.

Though mankind sinned and lost dominion of the earth to Satan, God in His mercy and wisdom introduced a grand plan of atonement for man's sins and the redemption of mankind from the dominion and influence of Satan's spiritual kingdom (also known as the kingdom of darkness); a plan that was ultimately accomplished in the earthly incarnation, ministry, death and resurrection of the Lord Jesus Christ. Jesus is the Second Person in the "triune God"—Father, Son and Holy Spirit—the Three-in-One God of the Christian faith.

Without the redemptive work of Christ according to the eternal plan of God, the fallen man that generationally descended from Adam and Eve would not have stood a chance of saving himself from the satanic kingdom, or of reclaiming authority and dominion over any part of the earth. But we, who have been redeemed by Christ Jesus, are privileged to incrementally recover, through our prevailing prayers, the dominion mandate over the earth that had been lost by Adam and Eve—and, quite significantly, partner with God in establishing His original will on earth.

In teaching His disciples how to pray, Jesus instructed them, among other things, to pray that the will of God be done on earth as it is done in heaven. God wants to partner with us to have His will established 100 percent in every aspect of the earth and in the lives of the people who dwell on it, as is the case in heaven. Ultimately, as the Bible explains, the full will of God will be totally accomplished on earth during the Second Coming of Jesus Christ to reign on earth—when Satan and all the forces of evil will be completely defeated and banished into hellfire, and when the present evil-infested world will pass away and a new, undefiled earth appear to replace the old.

Prayer and faith are like two sides of the same coin: "without faith it is impossible to please God" (*Hebrews 11:6, NIV*), including to prevail in prayer. It is faith in God's Word that empowers prayer to work. There is prevailing prayer, which must be prayed in faith: *prevailing faith*. "If there is a person to pray on earth," as many Pentecostal preachers have rhetorically captured it, "there is a God to answer in heaven."

In this book, prayer and faith are elucidated in their multiple facets and interconnections, so that believers in Christ can be thoroughly equipped for good works and effective prayer outcomes, in a world still largely dominated by the powers of darkness. The truth, which I wish to emphatically declare here, is that the kingdom of darkness is no match in spiritual power to any praying believer, church, or body of believers that understand the extraordinary greatness of God's power which is available to us who believe in Christ Jesus.

The Purpose of This Book

To have a new spiritual life in Christ is real, potent and impactful. Contrary to what many believe, that there are different ways to God, the Bible teaches that Jesus Christ is the only Way; otherwise, God would not have sent His Son Jesus to suffer such a brutal and shameful death for the sins of mankind. If there were other ways, God would have spared Jesus and simply allowed sinful humans to be reconciled to Him and earn eternal salvation through those other ways. This is why the most important prayer for anyone who has yet to experience God's salvation through accepting Jesus as personal Lord and Savior is the prayer for forgiveness of sins and reconciliation with God. This same prayer is equally important for any backslidden Christian who has strayed away from the Lord into spiritual darkness.

God is merciful, who has given us such a great salvation in Christ, that all who believe in Him, confess their sins, and call upon the name of the Lord will be saved. Like the prodigal son in the Bible, who recognized at a critical juncture in his life that he had sinned against heaven and earth and needed to return to his father to ask for mercy, anybody who wants to be reconciled or restored to God and obtain the free gift of salvation in Christ can pray the following prayer:

> *My heavenly Father, have mercy on me today and forgive all my sins. I believe Your Word, that You sent Jesus Christ, who took upon Himself the punishment of death that I deserve as a sinner, and that He rose again on the third day to give me a new life which cannot be subdued by the power of sin and death. I accept Jesus into my life (afresh) today as my personal Lord and Savior. Write my name in Your Book of Life and give me the grace to henceforth live a holy life, pleasing to God in all things, in Jesus' name. Amen.*

By saying this prayer wholeheartedly, anyone previously unsaved or backslidden from the kingdom of God will be saved and restored. In the words of the Lord Jesus in the Holy Bible, you are now born again, which is another way of saying that you have now become a spiritual child of God. Furthermore, if you are sick, and you have already said the above salvation prayer, you could add the following healing prayer to it, for God to extend His saving grace to heal your body:

Heal me, Lord, by your mercy, and I shall be healed. Deliver me from all the afflictions and diseases of the kingdom of darkness, in Jesus' name. Amen.

This book is conceivably beneficial to every reader and will be of even greater blessing to anyone who is a born-again child of God—including the person who at this moment has just received the Lord Jesus Christ as personal Lord and Savior. Make no mistake about it, life is fundamentally spiritual. Once you are born again into the kingdom of God, you no longer belong to the kingdom of darkness; and, consequently, you are now enlisted in the spiritual army of the Lord on earth. The satanic kingdom you have rejected and left behind could come after you, but if you hold on to the Lord Jesus and "learn the ropes" through diligent commitment to the sound doctrines of a Bible-believing church, Satan and his evil kingdom will not prevail.

I have included many relevant prayers in this book for the reader's benefit. It is pertinent to mention here that effective prayer is principally a Holy Spirit-guided and -directed activity, which could sometimes defy any pre-planned structures. The Bible tells us that we do not really know how to pray as we ought to, but the Holy Spirit helps our weaknesses in prayer because He knows the mind of God and can quicken us to pray effectually (*Romans 8:26*). So, it is essential that you depend on the Holy Spirit as you pray. Receiving the baptism of the Holy Spirit can also help to strengthen your prayer life, and you will learn how you can do so later in this book.

Finally, this book has been conceived to solve real-life problems. Therefore, it is my faith, prayer and conviction that God will use the knowledge and prayers contained within these pages to spiritually empower many readers and, in addition, to solve their practical problems. The problem-solving aspect, I humbly believe, will be a glorious testament to the divine purpose of the book.

Kenneth Omeje
Bradford, UK
info@crownofchrist.org.uk

PART 1

PREVAILING PRAYERS

Chapter 1

The Pervading Power of Prayer

Many years ago, I had the opportunity to counsel and pray for a certain young man concerning his career and marriage. He later got engaged to a young lady he met during a visit to his home country in Africa. It was love at first sight. When he returned to the UK and broke the good news of his engagement to me, I was truly delighted, especially on learning that his fiancée was a kindhearted and prayerful lady. During the engagement, she would always call him on the phone from Africa to pray with him first thing in the morning and also at bedtime.

The lady's prayer style was reportedly marked by Pentecostal fervour and militancy. She routinely expressed interest in her would-be husband's spiritual wellbeing, always probing into what spiritual activities he had engaged in within the week—church services, Bible studies, and the like. Up until this time, I had never spoken to the lady but, being a minister of the Gospel, I was elated over how she was passionately helping to uplift the young man's spiritual life—notwithstanding the logistical constraints of their being separated by the long distance between the UK and Africa. It was evident that the young man's spiritual life was being positively impacted.

After a reasonable period of courtship, they got married and the man subsequently returned to Africa to join his wife for good. But when they started living together as a married couple, the regular initiatives from the woman to pray and attend church activities were completely gone. The man was now the one urging her to pray but she would occasionally query, "What are we praying for? After all, God has already answered our prayers"—referring to their getting married. Her prayer life and spiritual zeal had plummeted, to the consternation of her husband.

From all indications, this young lady had meant well (in a natural sense), but she had genuinely misunderstood the purpose of prayer.

And she is not alone in this misconception. For many Christians, prayer is just an "emergency key" to apply when they want God to help them with a need or a problem. Once the need is met or the problem solved, they no longer see much purpose in prayer—or perhaps in sustaining the fervent prayer regime they once had when they desperately needed God's intervention.

This book sheds light on the power of prayer and how you can deploy your personal faith to prevail in prayer, surmount the challenges of life and, above all, sustain a healthy prayer life. Among other things, the book delves into the various types of prayers, why effective prayer is difficult for many Christians, the conditions for prayer to achieve the desired results, and the agency of the Holy Spirit in prayer.

Why do people have to pray, and Christians for that matter? "Prayer," writes Bonifes Adoyo, "is an acknowledgement that there is an invisible superior realm that affects the physical and visible world."[2] As the Bible explains, God created human beings and leased the earth to them, with the mandate to exercise dominion and authority over all things comprised on it and the responsibility to creatively tame, tend and transform it. Man was never created to execute his divine mandate on earth independent of God, but in partnership with and obedience to Him, in order to facilitate the establishment of God's divine will and purposes on earth.

The fall of the first humans, Adam and Eve, when they chose to obey the devil and disobey God's command, derailed the divine plan. God's renowned servant and great Bible teacher, Kenneth E. Hagin, described the spiritual transaction that happened in the biblical fall in this way: "Adam had dominion upon this earth and in the world. He was originally, in a sense, god of this world. But Satan came and lied to Adam. Adam committed high treason and sold out to Satan. Then Satan became the god of this world" (*Hagin, 2007:4*).

Under Satan's vicious dominion, the earth was filled with false religions, spiritual darkness, broken lives, misery, hardship, sexual perversion, disease, natural disaster, covetousness, violence, wars, death, and all forms of evil. God in His mercy commenced a remedial plan to redeem mankind from the bondage and wickedness of Satan and to restore to man the dominion mandate he had lost. God's remedial plan, executed over the millennia, included the inferior old covenant before Christ and the superior new covenant founded on the incarnation, atoning death and resurrection of Jesus Christ. God's remedial covenants are generally characterized by corresponding duties, obligations, commandments, sanctions, promises and blessings.

To access the various privileges and benefits in God's covenant provisions and remedial plan following the fall, diverse kinds of prayers became a requirement for God's mercy and supportive intervention. Consequently, under the superior new covenant between God and man, Jesus Christ provides access to all the promises and blessings of God, and He also guarantees answers to prayers (*Adoyo, 2006:1212*). The dominion mandate lost by Adam and Eve to Satan has been restored to mankind by Jesus Christ and, consequently, can only be executed through the redemption He freely offers and through faith in His name.

Prayer is the greatest power that God has entrusted to mankind for spiritual governance and for getting things done and exercising the restored dominion mandate over creation on this earth. Spiritual revival and diverse miracles from God happen because of prayer. Evil yokes are broken and people are set free from the clutches of Satan when we pray. All kinds of fears vanish and breakthroughs occur because of prayer. Prayer equips the children of God to resist and overcome temptations and live a victorious life. "Watch and pray, lest you enter into temptation," Jesus admonished His disciples (*Matthew 26:41*).

The more and longer we pray in line with God's will, the more we could possibly grow in spiritual power and in prophetic insights and revelations. The devil and the forces of darkness are rattled and terrified when holy men and women who know their God tarry persistently in prayer. It is in the place of prayer that we invite God to intervene in the events on earth because, by His order of creation, God has for a certain dispensation confined His jurisdiction of dominion to the highest heavens and, consequently, given or leased the earth to mankind (*Psalm 115:16*).[3] Prayer is the *major key* by which the redeemed of the Lord execute their restored dominion over the earth and against the continued countervailing contention of Satan and the fallen angels. This explains why Reverend John Wesley, the famous 18th century English Christian theologian and revivalist, reportedly declared: "It seems that God does nothing [*on earth*] except in response to believing prayer"—*in other words, the prayers of believers.*[4]

My definition of prayer in Christianity is two-pronged. Prayer is a means of communication and fellowship with God, as well as a weapon for enforcing the will of God here on earth, based on the scriptural authority given to the saints, exercised in the name of Jesus Christ. When we pray, we communicate with God in heaven in diverse ways and depths, some of which are beyond our human abilities, and that is why the Holy Spirit has been given to us individually upon our salvation to help us. He is the Spirit that raised Jesus from the dead, the Spirit of Christ who is in us (the hope of glory).

Further, through prayer, we can enter into fellowship with God the Father and His Son Jesus Christ, by the power and help of the indwelling Holy Spirit. As we fellowship with God in prayer, our spiritual strength is renewed and recharged for greater partnership work and exploits with God. Many Christians understand prayer as a means of communicating with God (and to a lesser extent, as fellowship with God), but not as a weapon for enforcing and establishing our restored dominion mandate on earth *by the authority vested in the name of Jesus Christ.*

God has highly exalted Jesus Christ, who is Himself ONE with God and who has atoned for the sins of the world through the perfect sacrifice He offered to God by His blood of the new covenant. And God has also exalted the name of Jesus above all other names in the universe in spiritual power and dominion.[5] The Person of Jesus Christ and the name of Jesus Christ are ONE and are extraordinarily powerful in the spiritual realm. Satan and the entire kingdom of darkness understand the great power in the name of Jesus, and they tremble and bow to the power in His name. Consequently, in the new covenant age which started about 2000 years ago, the highly exalted name of Jesus is the only authorized name under heaven by which God grants salvation to people and ultimately answers prayer.[6]

When Jesus appointed seventy disciples and sent them out on an evangelistic outreach before the atonement, they returned with joy and reported to the Lord, saying, "even the demons are subject to us in Your name" (*Luke 10:17*). In that first mission, the disciples were astonished at the great spiritual power vested in the name of Jesus; but in their subsequent missions after the death and resurrection of Jesus, those early disciples and other converts became accustomed to the glorious power in His name, freely using the name of Jesus to heal the sick, cast out demons, and raise the dead.

We exercise our dominion mandate in prayer or in scripturally-backed faith declarations in the name of Jesus Christ. By the power in His name, we are authorized to bind and prohibit whatever we disallow within our jurisdictions here on earth, and, moreover, to demand and command the things we desire to see manifested. All these must ultimately align with the will of God

By His total obedience to the will of God, even to the point of suffering the punishment of death on the cross on our behalf, Jesus restored to the church (believers in Christ) the dominion mandate to reign in life—a mandate that Adam and Eve had surrendered to Satan by their disobedience to God. Our restored dominion mandate *extends to all created things on earth, including Satan and his fallen angels, and all the things comprised in nature*. Hence, prayer is not only about speaking to God, but it also includes using the relevant words of the Holy Scriptures to speak to human problems and to command any spirits behind them to obedience in the name of Jesus.

In practice, the two dimensions of prayer are not mutually exclusive, but inclusive. There are times you could be communicating with God in prayers of thanksgiving, adoration, reverence, petition or intercession; but in the same space of time, you could also be launching into prayers of dominion and blocking of demonic agendas, depending on the diverse issues you are dealing with. These various dimensions of prayers could be gleaned from the famous "Our Lord's Prayer" taught by Jesus, which I have discussed in Chapter 4.

In the Gospels we see where Jesus, in exercising the dominion mandate, rebuked the wind and spoke to still the stormy sea on His boat journey with His disciples; and the sea was immediately calmed. Jesus spoke to the wind and the stormy sea by faith, as one who had divine authority over nature and creation. He did not pray. Indeed, most miracles that Jesus performed were accomplished by His spoken words of authority, as opposed to prayer. Elijah, on the other hand, achieved similar results *through prayer* when he withheld rain on the earth for three-and-half years (in his zeal to use drought and famine to turn King Ahab and the straying nation of Israel from worshipping Baal to the true God). On another occasion, Jesus cursed a blossoming but fruitless fig tree, and it dried up overnight. He used the incident to teach His disciples (and us) a lesson about the place of faith in exercising our dominion mandate, saying:

> Have faith in God. For assuredly, I say to you, whoever says to this mountain, "Be removed and be cast into the sea," and does not doubt in his heart, but believes that those things he says will be done, he will have whatever he says.
>
> *Mark 11:22-23*

By faith in God and His Word, we can speak to any mountain (meaning problem or obstacle in life), and the Spirit of God will compel it to bow to our dominion mandate, in the name of Jesus Christ. Impliedly, our restored dominion mandate is exercised through our submission to and partnership with God in Christ.

Prayer is the key to deploying our spiritual warfare weapons: "For the weapons of our warfare are not carnal, but mighty through God to the pulling down of strongholds" (*2 Corinthians 10:4, KJV*). We tend to underestimate the divine-fellowship dimension of prayer, and I shall elaborate on this later in this chapter. It is through the divine-fellowship dimension of prayer that we can dwell "in the secret place of the Most High" (*Psalm 91:1*).

The Bible contains many passages summoning Christians to the ministry of prayer, not just to pray for our own personal needs but to pray in line with the will of God. Impliedly, there are many types of prayers which, strictly, are not mutually exclusive. It suffices to cite a few of these Bible passages here:

> **Is anyone among you suffering? Let him pray...**
> *James 5:13*
>
> Then He spoke a parable to them, that **men always ought to pray and not lose heart**...
> *Luke 18:1*
>
> **Rejoice always, pray without ceasing**, in everything give thanks; for this is the will of God in Christ Jesus for you.
> *1 Thessalonians 5:16-18*
>
> And take the helmet of salvation, and the sword of the Spirit, which is the word of God; **praying always with all prayer and supplication in the Spirit, being watchful to this end with all perseverance and supplication for all the saints**...
> *Ephesians 6:17-18*

From the preceding scriptures, it is evident that prayer is a divine command. Prayer is a constant and daily necessity for living a victorious spiritual life. It is part of a believer's way of life, together with faith, holiness, love and good works, or the fruit of righteousness.

Prevailing Prayer

All Christians who pray practically desire to see the answers to their prayers granted and manifested by God at the earliest possible time. We are encouraged and gratified when our prayers achieve the desired results. Prevailing prayer is prayer that obtains the answer sought; it is an effective prayer that works, a prayer that obtains results or answers from God.[7] As further defined and explained by Charles Finney, America's great 19th century revivalist:

> Prevailing, or effectual prayer, is that prayer which attains the blessing that it seeks. It is that prayer which effectually moves God. When I speak of moving God, I do not mean that God's

mind is changed by prayer, or that His disposition or character is changed. But prayer produces such a change in us as renders it consistent for God to do as it would not be consistent for Him to do otherwise.[8]

In his time, Finney combined simple preaching of the Gospel with abundant prayers—in private, in social circles, and in public prayer meetings—to accomplish extensive conversion of sinners and revival of local churches, towns and communities.[9] Charles Finney was undoubtedly an apostle of selfless, prevailing prayer.

We are truly delighted and more motivated to pray when we prevail in our prayers and see needs being met and burdens lifted. As a minister of the gospel, I pray for people all the time. This is because so many people frequently contact me with their seemingly difficult problems, such as distressing medical diagnoses or severe attacks by unclean spirits (often manifesting as suicidal thoughts, self-harm, mental health issues, the hearing of strange voices or encounters with spirit spouses, and the like). In my characteristic faith declaration, I would calmly reassure them that Jesus would help them, occasionally citing examples of people with similar conditions whom I had prayed for and the Lord had healed. The latter I do, to boost the sufferers' faith in the lovingkindness and power of God. Most times, after I had prayed, the Lord would truly confirm their healing and deliverance. It always seemed effortless to me, because I hadn't done anything extraordinary to secure the results which they had earnestly desired. Just the grace of God!

Prevailing prayer does not always have to be laborious and gruelling, as many think, even though too often it could be. In the few cases where I prayed for someone and the expected miracle did not happen, I am always encouraged, by recalling previous positive results I have witnessed, to continue to pray, counsel and encourage the person, and believe for and command the desired outcomes.

About 16 years ago, for instance, I would fast for days, pray my heart out, quote all the relevant scriptures I knew for sick persons to be healed, but the results were seldom positive. Did I get discouraged then, by the insignificant results of my prayers for the sick? Not at all. I tried to encourage myself by faith in the Word of God and by the positive results some ministers of the gospel I knew firsthand were getting. I persevered. Evidently, by God's grace, we grow in spiritual capacity for prevailing prayers in different areas of life. I am still earnestly striving to grow.

Some gospel ministers would describe the observed growth in spiritual capacity for prevailing prayers as "personal anointing". One can have a genuine personal anointing or spiritual gift—or to speak more broadly, what could be simply called "grace"—for diverse worthy activities such as singing, teaching, healing, deliverance, working of miracles, administration or craftmanship, distributed according to God's own will to various children of His. But you have to earnestly and prayerfully desire spiritual gifts and God's supply or increase of grace in any area of need. Out of the fullness of Christ, says the Bible, have we all received one grace after another:

> And you know that God anointed Jesus of Nazareth with the Holy Spirit and with power. Then Jesus went around doing good and healing all who were oppressed by the devil, for God was with him.
>
> *Acts 10:38, NLT*

As born-again children of God, it is to our advantage to take personal responsibility to pray for our problems, especially when all possible external helps and schemes have failed. In fact, the sooner we take personal responsibility to gain appropriate spiritual knowledge and deploy the knowledge of the truth gained as an arsenal for spiritual warfare, the quicker the prospect of our prevailing in prayer.

From my many years of preaching and ministering to people as a servant of God, my observation is that taking personal prayer responsibility for their problems is one thing many Christians do not want to hear about or do. "God will do it if it pleases Him," they would say; or, "I need a highly-anointed man of God to pray for me, and it will all be sorted out," or, "I need a prophet who will reveal to me everything about this problem and pray to end it." Such a mindset is spiritually childish, anti-growth, and occasionally prolongs people's problems by delaying answers from heaven.

Under the present new covenant dispensation, when every born-again Christian has the indwelling Holy Spirit—the Spirit that raised Jesus from the dead—God desires every one of His children to take personal responsibility for the outcomes of their faith through the opportunities and diverse resources He has made available to them. For instance, in addition to the biblical doctrines of our respective local churches, we now have so much sound teaching freely available online, by way of sermons, publications and anointed prayers by seasoned servants of God, dead or alive, that could help to equip everyone who strives for personal spiritual responsibility.

"A baby has no responsibility at all," wrote American televangelist Joyce Meyer (*1995:2000*), "but as the child grows up, he is expected to take more and more responsibility." Learn to take responsibility for your problems and circumstances in life; don't outsource or delegate responsibility for your personal situation because that hardly works. Quit moaning and lamenting that there is no one to help you. Don't wallow in cynicism and self-pity. Stop the endless blame game—blaming all those who messed up your life and literally threw you into a waterless pit. I don't intend to sound insensitive and mean, but those responsible for your predicament may never come back to fix it or even have the ability to turn it around. Forgive them. To forgive is golden and liberating, just as God has forgiven us in Christ.

Most importantly, remember that the Most High God has saved you and given you the Holy Spirit, the greatest Helper you will ever need. God is faithful, and His revealed word in the Bible is dependable. There is no problem or temptation confronting anybody today that many steadfast believers have not overcome in the past. Even much bigger problems have been surmounted in the past through faith in God's Word. Hence, if you are determined to walk steadfastly with God, you will surely be victorious.

In writing or preaching about prevailing prayer, ministers of God often use the example of Jacob's overnight encounter with the angel of the Lord in Genesis 32 (when he journeyed back from Haran in Mesopotamia to Canaan). Greatly distressed and afraid that his brother Esau, whom he had robbed of his birthright some two decades earlier, was advancing with about 400 troops towards him and his defenceless mega-family, Jacob withdrew himself into an overnight solitary supplication. He prayed for God to deliver him and his large company from the hand of Esau, and that night a "man" wrestled with him (supposedly in a dream) until daybreak; but Jacob prevailed. Consequently, his supplication for supernatural blessing was granted by the spiritual personality he encountered, who declared to the victorious Jacob, "Your name shall no longer be called Jacob, but Israel; for you have struggled with God and with men, and have prevailed" (*Genesis 32:28*). Jacob and his travelling team were later to find favour with Esau, following this breakthrough in supplication.

Partly using Jacob's prevailing supplication, John Baros, Pastor of the Apostolic Faith Church in Medford, Oregon, gives us five key requirements for prevailing prayer. They can be paraphrased and summarized as follows:

Faith

Faith is essential because we cannot please God without having faith in His revealed word, in His omnipotent power, and in His immeasurable love and goodness. Approaching God with genuine faith will always elicit divine approval: as Abraham, who asked God to end his childlessness, demonstrated (see *Genesis 15:2-6*); and, so did the Syrophoenician woman who pleaded with Jesus to heal her demon-tormented daughter (see *Mark 7:24-30*).

Sincerity

To be effective, prevailing prayer must come from a sincere heart. Be focused and intentional when you pray, like the woman with the issue of blood, who touched the hem of Jesus' garment and was instantly healed (see *Luke 8:43-48*).

Obedience

Jacob apparently prevailed in his prayer for blessing and divine protection because his journey from Haran in Mesopotamia to the land of Canaan was in obedience to God's command:

> Then the LORD said to Jacob, "Return to the land of your fathers and to your family, and I will be with you."
>
> *Genesis 31:3*

When we are acting wisely, in obedience to God's instruction or command, our prayers for divine intervention concerning any threats or obstacles in our way are likely to achieve effective results.

Humility

Jacob had sent messengers ahead of him to Esau, with a humble request for his brother's favour:

> Speak thus to my lord Esau, "Thus your servant Jacob says: 'I have dwelt with Laban and stayed there until now. I have oxen, donkeys, flocks, and male and female servants; and I have sent to tell my lord, that I may find favour in your sight.'"
>
> *Genesis 32:4-5*

Esau did not respond with a "yes" or "no" answer to Jacob's request but instead mobilized 400 troops to start advancing towards his brother—a move that Jacob perceived as threatening, and he therefore launched into earnest, humble supplication to God. Throughout, Jacob had humbled himself before God and man; and so, God gave grace to him (*James 4:6*) and answered his prayer.

Persistence

The story in Genesis 32 shows that, before his overnight supplication, Jacob had previously prayed, asking God to deliver him and his travelling team from the hand of his brother Esau. When he did not have the peace of God in his heart concerning his safety in the midst of the foreboding threat, Jacob took his prayers further, launching into an overnight supplication. Persistence is a necessary key to prevailing in prayer, especially in circumstances where answers from God do not come easily (*Baros, 2019*).

The Primacy and Power of Prevailing Prayer

Jesus prayed more than any of His disciples and prevailed in all His cases. To start His ministry and fulfil His destiny, He went into the wilderness, where He fasted and prayed for forty days. Throughout His earthly ministry, when He had finished ministering in the daytime and all His disciples had gone home to sleep, Jesus often went up the mountain to pray. Finally, to finish His ministry, Jesus agonized in prayer in the Garden of Gethsemane for three hours, His sweat becoming like great drops of blood falling to the ground—this, at a time when His disciples could not pray with Him for even an hour.

By His practical examples and the extraordinary results that He achieved in His ministry in total obedience to the Father's will, Jesus demonstrated to us the importance and power of prayer. So much so that His disciples asked Him to teach them how to pray, and Jesus responded to their request (see *Luke 11:1-13*). Thank God that the disciples learned the primacy and power of prevailing prayer because, after Jesus was gone, they became fervent in prayer—tarrying for long hours in the upper room, praying for the promised Holy Spirit, praying down the angel of God on repeated occasions, and growing in the power of God.

God delights in the prayers of His saints and is always willing to answer them. The reason why many of our prayers are not answered has more to do with us than the sovereign will of God. God is a covenant keeper. He is committed by covenant to answer our prayers if we understand and follow His scriptural principles and commandments. How you pray matters, because there are prayers that produce results and prayers that do not. I will discuss them separately in the subsequent two chapters.

Box 1.1: Pause to actively pray these prayer pointers

1) My heavenly Father, have mercy on me, In Jesus Name (IJN).
2) Lord, thank you because you are a covenant-keeping God and you are committed to answering my prayers, IJN.
3) As I read this book, Lord, teach me the principles of prevailing prayer and prevailing faith, IJN.
4) By the superior power in the Blood of redemption, I bind and cast out all contrary powers resisting and dampening my prayer life, IJN.
5) Lord, may you release a fresh mantle of spiritual fire upon my prayer life, IJN.
6) My heavenly Father, thank you for answering all my prayers, IJN.

Chapter 2

Prayers That Will Not Receive Answers from God

The Bible makes it clear that there are circumstances under which God will not answer our prayers, notably:

(1) Praying in a state of sin without repentance

Let me provide a few Bible passages to substantiate this point:

> The LORD is far from the wicked,
> But He hears the prayer of the righteous.
> *Proverbs 15:29*

> One who turns away his ear from hearing the law,
> Even his prayer is an abomination.
> *Proverbs 28:9*

> Behold, the LORD's hand is not shortened, that it cannot save, or his ear dull, that it cannot hear; but your iniquities have made a separation between you and your God, and your sins have hidden his face from you so that he does not hear.
> *Isaiah 59:1-2 (RSV)*

> Now we know that God does not hear sinners; but if anyone is a worshiper of God and does His will, He hears him.
> *John 9:31*

It is clear from many scriptures that God does not answer the prayers of sinners—and, by sinners, I do not essentially mean those who are not born-again Christians. God is God of all, and He answers the prayers of all who fear Him. You do not have to be born again to fear God. There are many people who are not born again that have the fear of God—far more than some born-again Christians, which is a big irony because this is not supposed to be the case.

Cornelius, a centurion of the Italian Regiment, was not yet born again when his prayers and almsgiving ascended as a memorial before God, provoking an angelic visitation to him. *Acts 10:2* testified of Cornelius, that he was "a devout man and one who feared God with all his household, who gave alms generously to the people, and prayed to God always." I am not sure that heaven could bear such a glowing testimony of divine approval for many of us who are born-again Christians.

What happens when a sinner genuinely repents of his sinful ways? *Proverbs 28:13* tells us that, if he forsakes his sins, he will obtain mercy and God will answer his prayers. Now, people often ask: if God does not answer sinners, or if He only answers repentant sinners, why are some unrepentant sinners still prospering? This is where many Christians seem not to understand the nature of God and how prayers produce outcomes. Even though God does not answer the prayers of the wicked, they can still receive good things from Him—but not as an outcome of God answering their prayers. There are also sinners who make temporary progress in life by unrighteous means. We will examine all this more fully below.

Why do sinners receive favours from God or make progress in life?
I will provide three answers to this question, as follows:

(i) **The first point is that God is merciful to all** and therefore allows His rain to fall on both the land of the righteous and unrighteous, and His sun to shine on the evil and the good (*Matthew 5:45*). This means that anybody can receive good things from God, regardless of their religion, beliefs or prayer—or lack of prayer—because He is a merciful God. A wicked farmer who cultivates his farm and works hard on it will receive a great harvest, as much as a faithful child of God who follows the same occupational principles. You do not need to be a Christian for God to bless you with a good spouse, intelligent children, a happy marriage, a wonderful career, a lovely home, and other good things of life. That is why Jesus reminds us that the heavenly Father knows we need these good things of life, which the Gentiles also seek and receive (*Matthew 6:32-33*).

(ii) ***Secondly, Satan can empower sinners through familiar spirits and answer their prayers, disguising himself as the true God.*** Even diviners, magicians and sorcerers can produce positive results: we find one example of this in *Acts 16:16-18*, where a certain slave girl was possessed with a spirit of divination and brought her masters much profit through fortune-telling. The spirit behind her enterprise and whatever results she produced was not of God. Many flocked to her because she could foretell their fortunes, in the same manner that she accurately pronounced Apostle Paul and his team to be "the servants of the Most High God, who proclaim to us the way of salvation."

Moreover, sinners can amass wealth through drug peddling, robbery, bribe-taking, fraud, and the like. Many are never caught or punished for their crimes but continue to reap "the prosperity of the wicked" (*Psalm 73:3*). God is not behind such "prosperity" but Satan; and in *James 5:1-6*, God pronounces judgment on those who become rich by defrauding the labourers who work for them, keeping back their wages.

(iii) ***Thirdly, one living in sin or perhaps already judged by God can also receive blessings and miracles because of the prayers of the righteous***. *James 5:16* tells us, "The effective, fervent prayer of a righteous man avails much." *1 Kings 13* records the story of how a wicked king's hand was instantly paralyzed as part of God's judgment on his idolatrous reign, and how he was subsequently healed when he pleaded with a prophet of God to pray for him. God answered the prophet's prayer and healed the king's withered hand. Part of the story is as follows:

> King Jeroboam ... stretched out his hand from the altar, saying, "Arrest him!" Then his hand, which he stretched out toward him, withered, so that he could not pull it back to himself... Then the king answered and said to the man of God, "Please entreat the favour of the LORD your God, and pray for me, that my hand may be restored to me." So the man of God entreated the LORD, and the king's hand was restored to him, and became as before.
>
> *1 King 13:4, 6*

Having clarified the issue of why sinners can make material progress in life (even if temporarily), let us now turn to look at other possible reasons for our prayers going unanswered. Apart from praying in an unrepentant, sinful state, other circumstances under which we will not receive answers from God include:

(2) Praying amiss or praying with a wrong motive

> You ask and do not receive, because you ask amiss, that you may spend *it* on your pleasures. Adulterers and adulteresses! Do you not know that friendship with the world is enmity with God? Whoever therefore wants to be a friend of the world makes himself an enemy of God.
>
> *James 4:3-4*

God gives the good things of life to His children, but His primary purpose in blessing us is so that we might be channels of blessing to His kingdom affairs and to others. If we pray for and desire God's financial blessings with the motive, for instance, of indulging ourselves in a worldly fashion, like immoral fraudsters do, then we are misguided in our prayers; we could be praying amiss.

(3) Prayers of self-justification or self-exaltation

In His Parable of the Pharisee and the tax collector, Jesus gives us distinct examples of how to pray, and how *not* to pray:

> Two men went up to the temple to pray, one a Pharisee and the other a tax collector. The Pharisee stood and prayed thus with himself, "God, I thank You that I am not like other men—extortioners, unjust, adulterers, or even as this tax collector. I fast twice a week; I give tithes of all that I possess." And the tax collector, standing afar off, would not so much as raise *his* eyes to heaven, but beat his breast, saying, "God, be merciful to me a sinner!" I tell you, this man went down to his house justified *rather* than the other; for everyone who exalts himself will be humbled, and he who humbles himself will be exalted.
>
> *Luke 18:10-14*

The Pharisee missed it because his prayer was self-justifying and he foolishly recounted his righteous deeds, exalting himself above others, including the tax collector. The latter's prayer was an admission of guilt before God and a plea for mercy. The tax collector went home forgiven, justified and accepted by God, but not the Pharisee.

(4) Prayers of "faith" without corresponding works

A prayer of faith must be accompanied by corresponding works to produce the desired results. Faith is not mere words but Holy Spirit-charged words supported by action. For we walk by faith and not by sight, live by faith, work by faith, and talk by faith—all must align to produce a victorious Christian life. The faith that produces an excellent university graduation result, such as first-class honours, must be supported from day one in the university by diligence in attending lectures, completing all class assignments, sitting for all required exams, having a disciplined social life and constant personal study, and the like: "For as the body without the spirit is dead, so faith without works is dead also" (*James 2:26*).

I have come across many Christians who pray and talk with seemingly great "faith" about their impending breakthroughs—all without any kind of work plan. In fact, I know a few persons who resigned from their relatively well-paying jobs because of their "faith" in a revelation they purportedly received, that God had prepared a much better job for them or perfected plans to take them abroad to greener pastures. Meanwhile, they had no concrete plans about their next job or how to travel abroad, just wishful thinking and barren or dead faith. Invariably, these people ended up suffering for a long time, with no means of paying their bills or providing for their own sustenance.

When people are praying intensely and speaking words of faith without any accompanying works, they could even be dreaming seemingly positive dreams in accordance with their desires, which they easily interpret to mean that God is going to answer their prayers—yet the answers never show up. Most times, these dreams are not of God but generated by the human mind (the self) or by demons. Not all demonic dreams are terrifying, negative or scary.

The devil is a master deceiver and champion of pranks. He sometimes uses seemingly positive dreams to confuse people who "talk faith" (but without works) because they are not walking in wisdom. Anytime you are walking in folly and in ignorance of the scriptures, the devil could step in to feed you with deceptive, positive-looking dreams, purporting to indicate that you are headed in the right direction and will soon hit a breakthrough. By the time such people realize their folly and come to their senses, they may have lost many productive years on their empty "faith" confessions and, finding themselves in an untenable situation, might end up taking some unlawful way of escape offered by the devil. Do not accept any satanic or ungodly open door simply because you have been praying for an open door of opportunity for many years. Not all open doors are from God.

(5) Putting one's faith in a lying prophecy, dream or vision

Not all prophecies, dreams and visions are of God. In the spirit realm, there are too many voices speaking and issuing revelations to people, claiming to be of God; but many of them are lying tongues and the "revelations" could be from unclean spirits in their various disguises. If God has not, for instance, issued a certain prophecy that is purported to be from Him, and you put your faith in it, praying and expecting it to materialize, your expectations could amount to what the Bible calls "vain hopes" (*Jeremiah 23:16*). On the other hand, if God issues a terrifying warning of His impending judgment, calling for a quick repentance as a condition to avert His wrath, but you choose to pray against it— as opposed to genuinely repenting and asking for His mercy—His prophecy will surely overtake and devastate you.

During the time of the prophet Jeremiah, many false prophets were being regularly induced by the devil to counter every prophecy God gave Jeremiah for the benefit of the Jewish nation. Whenever the Lord inspired Jeremiah to prophesy to the people about His impending judgment on them, warning them that they would be carried off into captivity by the Babylonians because of their wicked ways, the devil instigated those lying prophets to prophesy perpetual peace to the people, telling them to disregard Jeremiah's prophecies.

Foolishly enough, the people chose to place their faith in the lying prophecies, as opposed to the true visions from God. The following verses in the Book of Jeremiah are instructive:

> They have lied about the LORD, and said, "*It is* not He. Neither will evil come upon us, nor shall we see sword or famine."
>
> *Jeremiah 5:12*

> Then I said, "Ah, Lord GOD! Behold, the prophets say to them, 'You shall not see the sword, nor shall you have famine, but I will give you assured peace in this place.'"
>
> *Jeremiah 14:13*

> As for the prophet who prophesies peace, when the word of that prophet comes to pass, then it will be known that the LORD has truly sent the prophet.
>
> *Jeremiah 28:9, RSV*

The Lord even warned the people not to believe those lying prophets, but they would not listen:

> Thus says the LORD of hosts: "Do not listen to the words of the prophets who prophesy to you, filling you with vain hopes; they speak visions of their own minds, not from the mouth of the LORD."
>
> *Jeremiah 23:16, RSV*

In the end, the prophecies of Jeremiah were fulfilled: the Jewish nation was invaded by the Babylonians and destroyed, with most of the people carried away into captivity.

We are seeing a prophetic awakening in this age as the Lord continues to pour out His Spirit, including the spirit of prophecy, upon all flesh and across many nations. Thank God for the spirit of prophecy; however, we need to test the spirits, whether they are of God. As in the days of Jeremiah, the devil is not resting but intensifying the activities of familiar spirits and, especially, the spirit of divination. These spirits are all in the Church today, issuing diverse prophecies—with the result that many Christians are excited, and some are confused.

I have seen too many naïve Christians being misguided and manipulated by the abuse of prophecies and visions of "Thus says the Lord." On more than one occasion, the Holy Spirit has prompted me to leave a church or switch off a "Christian" TV broadcast because the prophetic spirit behind it was of a contrary source. On each occasion, I have felt great sympathy and compassion for the multitude of people in the audience who may not have the discerning grace to understand the operating spirit behind the façade. The Apostle John did warn the Church:

> Beloved, do not believe every spirit, but test the spirits, whether they are of God; because many false prophets have gone out into the world.
>
> *1 John 4:1*

We all need to constantly pray and grow in our capacity to test every spirit by the written Word of God and the discerning power of the Holy Spirit. As we grow in the Lord and in sensitivity to the Holy Spirit's leading, the true prophecies of God delivered to us by His chosen vessels will often come as a confirmation of things already spoken or revealed to us by the Lord.

Box 2.1: Pause to actively pray these prayer pointers

1) Lord, teach me how to pray by the help and power of the Holy Spirit; transform my prayer life, IJN.
2) Lord, empower me to pray and never to lose heart concerning my condition and my family's condition, IJN.
3) Lord, give me the wisdom to know how to back up my faith with corresponding works for maximum results, IJN.
4) Holy Spirit, deliver me from praying amiss and praying with the wrong motives, IJN.
5) Prayer-answering God, end my suffering today, IJN.
6) Lord, heal me and I shall be healed; make me whole indeed, IJN.

Chapter 3

Prayers That Will Receive Answers from God

The Bible does give us an idea of prayers that *will* receive answers from God—in contrast to the prayers that God will not respond to—so that we are not left perplexed as to how to get our prayers answered. Many leading Bible scholars have written about this subject of prayers that will receive answers from God. For example, God's servant Derek Prince (2009:23-54) has outlined and discussed eight basic conditions for getting our prayers answered, which I have paraphrased as follows:

(1) **Come with reverent submission** to the will of God, renouncing your own will and embracing His will for you.

(2) **Have faith in God**, because anyone who comes to God must believe that He exists and that He rewards those who earnestly seek Him.

(3) **Pray in the name of Jesus**, the only name that God has exalted and given under the heavens by which salvation is proclaimed and prayers answered. Jesus has confirmed to His disciples that, if we ask the Father anything in His name, it will be given to us.

(4) **Approach God boldly**, with confidence that He is a merciful, prayer-answering Father. Come without condemnation relating to any confessed sins. We should not carry the consciousness of sin into our prayers because, once we have repented of our sins and confessed them, God is faithful to forgive and sanctify us.

(5) **Come with the right motive**, understanding that God searches our hearts to judge the motives behind everything we do or pray for. Wrongly motivated prayers will not be answered. The right motive in praying should be that the answer brings glory to God.

*(6) **Forgive those who have hurt you*** because, if you do not, God will neither forgive you nor deliver you from the evil one, and your prayers will be blocked and not be answered.

*(7) **Be directed by the Holy Spirit**,* who helps us in our weaknesses in prayer and enables us to pray according to the revealed will of God.

*(8) **Ask according to God's Word**,* for God's will is contained in His Word, and we know from Scripture that, when we pray according to God's will, He hears us. And if we know that God hears us, then we know that He has answered our petitions.

These eight scriptural requirements enumerated by Derek Prince are right on point. In one of his several lectures on the characteristics of effectual or prevailing prayers, the 19th century American revivalist Charles Finney cited practically all the prerequisites highlighted by Derek Prince above. However, Finney added that what is essential, for us to prevail in prayer and receive answers from God, is object-focused, persevering prayer.[10] To be object-focused simply means that our prayer is not aimless but purposeful and that we are passionate about praying for the intended purpose.

Let me now take this discussion a step further, as I invite my readers to join me on a quest; and our aim is to discover the essentials we need to have, for our prayers to receive answers from God.

(1) The effective, fervent prayer of the righteous avails much

Prayer is a spiritual activity. The God we pray to is Spirit, and the born-again believer engaging in prayer is fundamentally a spirit being who lives in a human body and has a soul. The Holy Spirit, who dwells in the heart of every believer, helps us to overcome our natural weaknesses and achieve effective results when we engage in earnest prayer. The effectiveness or efficacy of the prayer of the righteous is explained in the following Bible passage:

> [16] Confess *your* trespasses to one another, and pray for one another, that you may be healed. **The effective, fervent prayer of a righteous man avails much.** [17] Elijah was a man with a nature like ours, and he prayed earnestly that it would not rain;

and it did not rain on the land for three years and six months. ¹⁸ And he prayed again, and the heaven gave rain, and the earth produced its fruit.

James 5:16-18

The phrase, "the effective, fervent prayer of a righteous man," which Apostle James used in verse 16 above, is further rendered in verse 17 as "earnest prayer"—using the example of Elijah, a righteous prophet of God. Some Bible commentaries have further explained "the effective, fervent prayer of the righteous" to mean "the Holy Spirit-inspired prayer" or "the Holy Spirit-energized prayer" of a God-fearing believer who is the righteousness of God in Christ.[11] The Amplified Bible translates the phrase as "the heartfelt and persistent prayer of a righteous man (believer)".

The "earnest prayer" of Elijah, as Apostle James recounted in the preceding Bible passage, achieved the extraordinary result of withholding rain on the earth for three and a half years; and the writer assures us that "the effective, fervent prayer" of any righteous person can accomplish just as much in the way of desired results. When we pray, it is important to recognize that prayer grows in intensity or frequency. The Holy Spirit helps the children of God to take prayer to higher frequencies and, in the process, aligns our prayers with the will of God because the Holy Spirit searches all things, including the deep things of God.

The Bible offers several examples of the "earnest prayer of the righteous" availing much by way of result. It suffices to mention only the prayer of Jesus Christ ahead of the looming agony of His death by crucifixion:

> ⁴¹ And He was withdrawn from them about a stone's throw, and He knelt down and prayed, ⁴² saying, "Father, if it is Your will, take this cup away from Me; nevertheless not My will, but Yours, be done." ⁴³ Then an angel appeared to Him from heaven, strengthening Him. **⁴⁴ And being in agony, He prayed more earnestly. Then His sweat became like great drops of blood falling down to the ground.**
>
> *Luke 22:41-44*

Did God answer this agonized, earnest prayer of Jesus? The answer is YES. God answered the prayer in line with His will for Christ Jesus—or, put differently, in accordance with the eternal resolution and foreknowledge of the Trinity, which includes Jesus as the Second Person in the Godhead. Verse 43 says that "an angel appeared to Him from heaven, strengthening Him". Any prayer that provokes an angelic intervention or visitation from Heaven has received an answer from God. Furthermore, *Hebrews 5:7* tells us that "in the days of His flesh, when He [Jesus] had offered up prayers and supplications, with vehement cries and tears to Him who was able to save Him from death… [He] was heard because of His godly fear".

(2) Praying with importunity and thanksgiving

Importunity means persistence to the point of provoking anger and annoyance. Importunity is an expression of a defiant faith. As a child of God, you need defiant faith, boldness, and resilience in prayer to secure what is rightfully your heritage according to God's will and, where necessary, to resist the countervailing forces of the adversary. As Patrick Regan (2021:10) puts it: "More than education, more than experience, more than training, a person's level of resilience will determine who succeeds and who fails. That's true in the cancer ward, it's true in the Olympics, and it's true in the boardroom." Our resilience, as children of God, is based on our faith in the integrity of His Word.

Too often, when God opens a door of blessings to His children, they find themselves up against many adversaries assigned by the kingdom of darkness to block or shut that open door. Praying with importunity means that you don't give God a rest—and also, that you don't give Satan a chance—until you receive those blessings.

In the Gospel of Luke, Jesus teaches us how effective the prayer of importunity could be and consequently instructs us to ask, seek and knock—all with importunity—and the answer will be ours to enjoy:

> And he said unto them, Which of you shall have a friend, **and shall go unto him at midnight**, and say unto him, Friend, lend me three loaves, for a friend of mine in his journey is come to me, and I have nothing to set before him?

And he from within shall answer and say, Trouble me not: **the door is now shut, and my children are with me in bed; I cannot rise and give thee. I say unto you, though he will not rise and give him, because he is his friend, yet because of his importunity he will rise and give him as many as he needeth.**

And I say unto you, Ask, and it shall be given you; seek, and ye shall find; knock, and it shall be opened unto you. For everyone that asketh receiveth; and he that seeketh findeth; and to him that knocketh it shall be opened.

If a son shall ask bread of any of you that is a father, will he give him a stone? or if he asks a fish, will he for a fish give him a serpent? Or if he shall ask for an egg, will he offer him a scorpion? If ye then, being evil, know how to give good gifts unto your children: how much more shall your heavenly Father give the Holy Spirit to them that ask him?

Luke 11:5-13, KJV

One thing which, to me, stands out in the narrative above is that the fellow who pestered his friend for bread did so *at midnight*, persisted *at midnight*, and his friend—who would not rise to help him because he had already gone to bed with his children—eventually rose *at that midnight* to give him as many loaves as he needed. The entire importunity happened *at that one midnight* and achieved the desired result. I will discuss this in more detail below. Meanwhile, let us look at how thanksgiving, when it is coupled with importunity, can add potency to our prayers.

All prayers, including prayers of importunity, are more effective when we *give prior thanks to God by faith*, believing that we have received the answers to our prayers. "Be anxious for nothing," the Apostle Paul exhorts us, "but in everything by prayer and supplication, **with thanksgiving**, let your requests be made known to God" (*Philippians 4:6*).

We give thanks to God because we believe He has already answered our prayers. "Therefore, I say to you," Jesus declared, "whatever things you ask when you pray, **believe that you receive *them*, and you will have *them*"** (*Mark 11:24*).

You have to continue in your prayers of thanksgiving, praising God for the answer, until the Lord manifests it in the physical realm. To persist in thanksgiving prayer prior to the physical manifestation of your expected desire is an act of defiant faith. By the same token, it is helpful to continue in midnight prayer, not only thanking God for the expected outcome, but also blocking and disallowing every agenda and legal ground of the kingdom of darkness concerning your awaited miracle.

Midnight supplication is highly effective, apparently because that is the time when the activities of the kingdom of darkness are most intense. In His parable of the wheat and the tares, Jesus likened the kingdom of heaven to "a man who sowed good seed in his field; but while men slept, his enemy came and sowed tares among the wheat and went his way" (see *Matthew 13:24-30*). Midnight prayers are important for stopping the devil from sowing tares in people's lives and in the kingdom of God, and for rooting out the evil he has already sown.

Acts 16 tells us that Paul and Silas prayed and sang hymns to God at midnight while they were imprisoned. Suddenly the Lord sent a great earthquake that shook the foundations of the prison, shattered all their fetters and flung open all the prison doors. Their midnight prayers had provoked a great deliverance for them. I have done midnight prayers for about 30 years, and I have seen its effective results, both in my personal life and in the lives of the many people for whom I have interceded.

A remarkable result I personally secured during my first decade of midnight prayers was the healing of a chronic affliction on the back of my head, medically known as "acne keloidalis nuchae" (AKN). I had those painful, itchy and disfiguring scalp lesions, which frequently bled during my sleep and after showering.[12] The affliction started suddenly about eight years before I got saved. I couldn't really put my finger on what triggered it—possibly from one of the casual haircuts I often received as a teenager at some local barber shops with doubtful hygiene conditions. For years, it defied all the treatments prescribed by various local doctors I consulted.

My dad tried to encourage me by saying that, when he was a young man, he had a less chronic version of the same infection that had also defied medical treatment for many years. He bought for me a certain dermatological cream that had eventually cured his own AKN. With much excitement and hope, I applied the cream, but the medication proved unhelpful to me.

Even after I became born again in August 1991, this back-head affliction defied all prayers and laying on of hands by anointed servants of God for the next couple of years. Possibly, there could have been a gifted servant of God somewhere in the uttermost parts of the earth, whose anointed prayer could have healed me at once, but I was not privileged to meet him or her. The ones I was privileged to meet, highly anointed as they were, had done their best, and I remain grateful for all their prayers.

All subsequent medical treatments I received from dermatologists and other skincare specialists during my postgraduate study and research fellowship years in Austria and the United States between 1992 and 1994 only aggravated the condition, spreading the itchy lesions all over my head and causing frequent hair loss.

When every medical and external spiritual intervention I sought had seemingly failed, I felt that this was my own equivalent of the intractable personal ailment that Paul described in *2 Corinthians 12:7* as "a thorn in the flesh" and "a messenger of Satan", given to torment him because of "the abundance of the revelations" he had received, so that he should not "be exalted above measure". But unlike Paul, I had not received an abundance of revelations; yet, I had this messenger of Satan buffeting me day and night!

Concerning his own affliction, Paul had pleaded with the Lord three times that it might depart from him. But the Lord's reply to him was: "My grace is sufficient for you, for My strength is made perfect in weakness" (*2 Corinthians 12:9*). I then resolved by faith never to seek any further help anywhere, but to deal with this "messenger of Satan" through my own prayers, largely midnight prayers, confident that His grace would be sufficient for me too. I spent hours from week to week, binding and banishing the wicked demon spirits behind the infirmity, breaking every known curse and evil yoke, and claiming supernatural healing based on the promises in relevant scriptures and by the power invested in the name of Jesus Christ. I was not systematic in my approach; I simply had a defiant mindset and an "enough-is-enough" combative resolve. In many dreams and night visions during the first three years of my midnight prayers, I encountered the obnoxious spirits or messengers of Satan behind the affliction, as they fought back and put up a stubborn resistance in various guises.

In the fourth year, healing gradually started and, within twelve months, all the symptoms, bumps and scars of AKN totally disappeared from my head. I was completely healed after four years of intense midnight prayers against the buffeting powers of darkness. Clearly, Jesus has given us authority over spiritual serpents and scorpions, and over all the powers of the enemy; but sometimes, and for certain deep-rooted demonic problems, it may take a long-drawn-out spiritual battle to secure victory.

The preceding case of my personal affliction raises a highly controversial question in Christendom—can a born-again Christian have a demon or be demon-possessed? I have addressed this issue in greater detail in a different book titled *Self-Deliverance Through Prayers*. However, it suffices to simply remark here that a true believer cannot be demon-possessed because he belongs to God and has the indwelling Holy Spirit in his spirit as a seal of his salvation. The reality of our modern times is that demon-possession is a highly uncomfortable term and attribution for everyone, believers and unbelievers alike. In fact, some reputable preachers have even argued that the reference to demon possession in various English translations of the Bible is a mistranslation (although it is not my place to question the authenticity of any Bible translation).

Because it is generally considered to be an objectionable, even offensive epithet, I am extremely reluctant to use the term "demon-possession" for anyone. You do not necessarily need to tell people that they are demon-possessed before you can help them overcome their distress or expel the demons troubling them. Jesus did not go about telling His clients that they were demon-possessed, but he effectively rebuked and expelled the demons that troubled them.

Many Bible teachers define demon possession to imply "full control or ownership by the devil". Not even those serving the devil would readily admit that a demon has full ownership or control over them.

From the Bible's standpoint, the human personality comprises three components—spirit, soul and body (*1 Thessalonians 5:23*) — with a complex interrelationship existing between these three. Whilst a demon cannot indwell the spirit of a true believer whose spirit is indwelt by the Holy Spirit, it is possible for demons to oppress, afflict, torment and buffet a believer's body or mind. Some Bible scholars describe this troubling experience, which could be severe in some cases, as demonization. By God's grace, I have prayed for many Christians troubled in diverse ways by unclean spirits, and the Lord delivered them. In prayers of importunity, you *do not* give any chance or opportunity to the devil or any unclean spirit; and furthermore, you *do not* concede any ground for permanent victory to them.

The Bible warns us about the activities of wicked human messengers of darkness (such as witches, warlocks and sorcerers) who cannot sleep at night unless they do evil, and who are deprived of sleep (by their master, the devil) unless they make someone stumble and fall: see *Proverbs 4:14-17*, AMP. Sometime in 2016, a young African lady who was married to a Caucasian man came to me, asking for prayers for her mother-in-law, who was waiting to undergo surgery for cancer; and because the prognosis wasn't looking good, the doctor had given her a 50–50 chance of survival. The lady and her entire family were Roman Catholics.

I assured her that Jesus would make the surgery hitch-free and effective, and I further advised her to join us in our weekly prayers as much as possible, so that we could intercede together for her mother-in-law. Immediately, she started joining us in our church activities, including our weekly Friday night vigil, which was from 9.00pm to 1.00am in those days. After a couple of weeks of prayer, the surgery was successfully performed and the mother-in-law made a rapid recovery, to the utter amazement of the doctor. She was discharged from the hospital and returned home to recuperate.

The week after the woman's successful surgery, I was preparing for our weekly night vigil on a Friday afternoon when the Holy Spirit said to me, "Pray against witchcraft attacks." I quickly prepared teaching materials on sorcery and witchcraft, sourced from the Bible, to guide us in our prayers against any attacks. That night, I announced to the people attending the vigil what the Holy Spirit had instructed me to do. After my exhortation, we prayed fervently, shielding all our church and family members from the evil enterprises of sorcerers and witches, disarming them, and issuing restraining orders against them. Unfortunately, the lady whose mother-in-law had recently undergone successful surgery was not in attendance that night. She later told me that, as she was preparing to come to the night vigil, she felt a strong, unexplainable force holding her back; and so, she stayed home.

The next morning, around 7.30am, she called me on the phone to report that her mother-in-law had just suddenly died, and she attributed her death to a witchcraft attack. This older woman, together with her husband, had gone peacefully to bed the previous night, and she had been in a stable, recovering condition then. But at dawn she woke up abruptly from her sleep, screaming violently in agonizing pain and gasping for breath. Overwhelmed with anguish, she narrated to her shocked husband how a former friend of hers, with whom she had had a strained relationship, had appeared to her in a dream, raging about how she (the ex-friend) had tried to kill her by afflicting her with cancer but was perplexed as to how she had survived it. In the dream, the furious assailant told the woman that, though she had survived the cancer, she was still determined to kill her, and she began stabbing the woman all over her body. There were no physical stab-wounds on the woman's body, but she quickly slipped into a coma. She was rushed to the hospital in those early hours of the morning but was pronounced dead shortly upon arrival there.

On hearing the sad news, I was devastated. The death could have been averted, had the young lady attended our vigil the previous night, as she had done regularly on all those other nights when her mother-in-law was awaiting surgery. The Holy Spirit had already forewarned us, and those attending the vigil had spent the night prayerfully shielding their family and our ministry members from witchcraft attacks. I tried to comfort the young lady a few times through my telephone calls, but she never came to our church again.

(3) Praying according to our knowledge of God's will and God's Word

God's will is contained in His Word, the Holy Scriptures; and as such, the prayer that brings effective results must be based on and supported by relevant scriptures. God is committed to answering prayers made in line with His will on earth. Jesus asked us to pray for God's will to be done on earth, but many Christians do not know God's will, whilst others are not passionate about praying for it. In teaching His disciples how to pray, this was how Jesus put it:

> When you are praying, do not heap up empty phrases as the Gentiles do; for they think that they will be heard because of their many words. Do not be like them, **for your Father knows what you need before you ask him**. Pray then in this way: Our Father in heaven, hallowed be your name. Your kingdom come. **Your will be done, on earth as it is in heaven**.
>
> Matthew 6:7-10, NRSVA

Two things are particularly instructive from the above pattern of prayer that Jesus taught His disciples. The first is that our heavenly Father already knows what we need before we ask Him and therefore, by implication, we should not overload our prayers with our own needs. Throughout nearly the first half of this prayer taught by Jesus, there is no mention of personal needs. Personal needs like "give us this day our daily bread," are featured only in the second half of the prayer.

The second point is that Jesus requires us to pray for God's kingdom to come and for His will to be done on earth as it is in heaven. God's will is done fully in heaven, and He wants His will to be done similarly on earth. But our prayers are required to facilitate this, and that is why Jesus commanded that we should pray for it. The establishment of the kingdom and will of God on earth is being resisted and subverted by the forces of darkness; hence, we need to pray and to preach the gospel of Christ to counter the adversary's resistance and reclaim peoples and territories for God. We need a combination of prayer and the teaching of God's Word for Christians and the church to align with God's will and passionately do His will.

The more the will of the adversary is overthrown and mitigated, and conversely the will of God advanced and executed, the better a place the earth would become. The Bible makes it clear that, if we pray according to the will of God on earth, He hears and answers us:

> And this is the confidence which we have in him, that if we ask anything according to his will, he hears us. And if we know that he hears us in whatever we ask, we know that we have obtained the requests made of him.
>
> *1 John 5:14-15, RSV*

It is possible to pray and know in the spirit or by faith that God has heard us and that we have received His answer because we are confident that we have prayed according to His will. Conversely, if we pray outside of God's will, He is less likely to answer us—even if we have prayed fervently.

In *2 Samuel 12*, God revealed through the prophet Nathan that the child David wrongfully had with Uriah's wife Bathsheba would die; and, subsequently, the child became very sick. David fasted and prayed for seven days for God to heal the baby boy, but he died on the seventh day. Ordinarily, it is in line with God's general will to answer a prayer of faith made by the righteous for the sick, an innocent sick child for that matter. But on this occasion, God did not answer David because He had already revealed His judgment (circumstantial will) that this child would die as one of the penalties for David's grievous sins of adultery, killing of Bathsheba's husband Uriah to cover up his iniquity, and unlawful acquisition of Uriah's wife.

Was David right in fasting and praying for seven days, despite knowing God's judgment that the child would not live but die? Absolutely YES. David persuasively explained why he prayed and fasted for the child, saying, "While the child was still alive, I fasted and wept; for I thought, 'Who knows, the Lord may be gracious to me and the child may live'" (*2 Samuel 12:22, AMP*). Even though David did not prevail in his prayers on this occasion, God graciously honoured his faith—because the next child he had with Bathsheba was Solomon, who found great favour with God and was divinely chosen to succeed his father as king over Israel.

Many Christians struggle with knowing the will of God and, hence, are less motivated to pray and work for it—unaware that the Bible has unequivocally delineated God's will on earth, which should guide our prayers and activities as God's children and the church of Jesus Christ. Listed below are specific examples of scriptural prayers that are in line with God's will, and this list is by no means exhaustive.

Praying in Accordance with God's Will: Examples

(i) ***Praying for the salvation of sinners:*** The primary reason God sent Jesus into the world was to extend salvation to mankind. This salvation is obtainable by all who repent of their evil works and accept Jesus Christ as their personal Lord and Saviour. The Bible tells us: "For God so loved the world, that he gave his only Son, that whoever believes in him should not perish but have eternal life" (*John 3:16, RSV*). Hence, every activity directed towards the salvation of an unredeemed person is in line with God's will. Such activities include fasting and prayer, preaching and teaching the gospel, handing out gospel tracts, giving money to an evangelical church or ministry that is practically committed to soul-winning, and so forth.

How many times have we fasted and prayed for the salvation of our unsaved family members, relatives, schoolmates, workmates and acquaintances? If we apply the principle of importunity in fasting and praying for their salvation, God will answer us and deliver them from the kingdom of darkness. This is in line with the will of God, who is forbearing and compassionate and does not wish that anybody should perish eternally in hell:

> The Lord does not delay [as though He were unable to act] and is not slow about His promise, as some count slowness, but is [extraordinarily] patient toward you, not wishing for any to perish but for all to come to repentance.
> *2 Peter 3:9, AMP*

A highly important but often neglected aspect of praying for the salvation of sinners is praying to break the stranglehold of the devil over them and to destroy the veils of satanic deception.

God has already done everything in Christ Jesus for any unbeliever to be saved. What is principally keeping unbelievers away from the grace of salvation is satanic deception through the veiling of their minds and the bondage of sin. Satan is described in the Bible as "the god of this world" who has "blinded the minds of them which believe not, lest the light of the glorious gospel of Christ, who is the image of God, should shine unto them" (*2 Corinthians 4:4 KJV*).

Reverend Kenneth Hagin preached and wrote about how quickly his unredeemed brother got saved the moment he (Hagin) changed his prayer strategy from fasting and praying that God would save him (which he had done repeatedly for 15 years) to breaking the power of the devil over him. Hagin's more effective prayer was: "In the name of the Lord Jesus Christ, I break the power of the devil over my brother Dub's life, and I claim his deliverance… And I claim his full salvation in the name of the Lord Jesus Christ" (Hagin, 2007:59). Within three weeks of executing his new prayer strategy, as Hagin reported, his brother gave his life to Christ and was born again.

(ii) ***Praying for the repentance of the righteous from their evil ways:*** Many Christians understand the need for the unrighteous to repent and obtain salvation but not the need for the repentance of the righteous (those already saved) from their evil schemes and satanic deceptions. The kingdom of darkness does not leave the righteous alone but at any cost wants to overcome them with temptations—and consequently make them live in besetting sin, believe and practise heresies, bring shame to the Lord and, if possible, ultimately miss eternal life. This is why the church must be as concerned about the redeemed of the Lord who are not living a victorious Christian life, as much as they are about the unsaved.

Occasionally, we see troubling headlines in the news about priests committing sins of sexual immorality, fraud, deception, and spousal abuse in marriages. If these things happen to the clergy, they could be even more rampant among the congregants.

It is all an indication of the spiritual battle that the adversary is waging against the church. We can prevent and mitigate such spiritual attacks by prayer, fasting, empathy and compassionate restoration of the struggling and the fallen. The Bible exhorts us:

> Dear brothers and sisters, if another believer is overcome by some sin, you who are godly should gently and humbly help that person back onto the right path. And be careful not to fall into the same temptation yourself. Share each other's burdens, and in this way obey the law of Christ. If you think you are too important to help someone, you are only fooling yourself. You are not that important.
>
> *Galatians 6:1-3, NLT*

(iii) ***Praying for the baptism and gifts of the Holy Spirit:*** Jesus told His disciples that, on His departure, He would ask the Father to send them the Holy Spirit to be their spiritual counsellor, teacher and comforter. The Holy Spirit is the third person in the Godhead and a gift to the church. When Jesus told His disciples, "Without me, you can do nothing" (*John 15:5*), He was referring to the abiding presence, ministry and power of the Holy Spirit. After His resurrection, Jesus instructed His disciples not to venture out of Jerusalem until they received the promised Holy Spirit, who would be their source of power in advancing the kingdom of God.

In Acts 2, we see the spectacular coming of the Holy Spirit, His baptism of fire upon the disciples who were praying in the upper room, and the commencement of the church age through the power and work of the Holy Spirit. The disciples' prayers brought down the Holy Spirit in power and fire, and it was the Holy Spirit who transformed their lives and ministries. Praying similar prayers today is perfectly in accord with the will of God for us. This is how Jesus prioritized the gift of the Holy Spirit:

> And I tell you, Ask, and it will be given to you; seek, and you will find; knock, and it will be opened to you. For everyone who asks receives, and the one who seeks finds, and to the one who knocks it will be opened.

> What father among you, if his son asks for a fish, will instead of a fish give him a serpent; or if he asks for an egg, will give him a scorpion? If you then, who are evil, know how to give good gifts to your children, **how much more will the heavenly Father give the Holy Spirit to those who ask him!**
>
> *Luke 11:9-13, RSV*

In a nutshell: asking the Father for the Holy Spirit *is* God's will, for He *wants* to give us the Holy Spirit. There are many things we can ask for in the Holy Spirit: His indwelling presence, His daily in-filling, His power, His baptism of fire, His baptism of speaking in tongues, His wisdom, and His variety of gifts distributed to the church for the profit of all (*1 Corinthians 12*).

We need to pray for the gifts of the Holy Spirit to abound in the church and for us to grow in grace in the manifestation and use of specific gifts we have already received for the purpose of serving God and humanity. If you have just one gift of the Holy Spirit, such as the gift of supernatural healing, and you are using it effectively to serve and advance the kingdom of God, it will attract answers to most of your personal prayer requests.

(iv) ***Praying for your own sanctification***: Sanctification is the act of making somebody holy—in spirit, soul and body. Your personal sanctification is God's will for you, and it is important to pray for it and walk daily in it, that you may continue to live in holiness:

> **For this is the will of God, your sanctification:** that you should abstain from sexual immorality; that each of you should know how to possess his own vessel in sanctification and honour, not in passion of lust, like the Gentiles who do not know God; that no one should take advantage of and defraud his brother in this matter, because the Lord *is* the avenger of all such, as we also forewarned you and testified. For God did not call us to uncleanness, but in holiness. Therefore he who rejects *this* does not reject man, but God, who has also given us His Holy Spirit.
>
> *1 Thessalonians 4:3-8*

Growing in sanctification, consecration and godliness is what makes us more and more like Jesus Christ, which is God's will for every child of God. How do you know when you are growing in sanctification? It is when you no longer struggle to think holy, speak holy, act holy or dress holy, but you do the will of God and meditate constantly on what the Word of God says concerning any matter, instead of meditating on the scale or longevity of your problem. We all need to grow in sanctification daily.

(v) ***Praying for the harvest of souls on earth and for more harvesters***: God wants His kingdom on earth to be populated with as many redeemed souls as possible. Jesus died for the sins of the whole world and, therefore, God wants to see the whole world saved if possible. The redeemed are called to the task of global soul-winning, that as many as possible may be saved. It is the prayers and soul-winning endeavours of the saints here on earth, working of course in partnership with the Holy Spirit, that will increase the possibility of salvation for many. Jesus saved and appointed us as His channels for the salvation of the lost:

> You did not choose Me, but I chose you and appointed you that you should go and bear fruit, and *that* your fruit should remain, that whatever you ask the Father in My name He may give you.
>
> John 15:16

Furthermore, Jesus specifically required His disciples to pray to the Lord to send more soul-winners into different parts of the world for the harvest of souls:

> When he saw the crowds, he had compassion for them, because they were harassed and helpless, like sheep without a shepherd. Then he said to his disciples, "The harvest is plentiful, but the laborers are few; **therefore pray earnestly to the Lord of the harvest to send out laborers into his harvest.**"
>
> Matthew 9:36-38, RSV

If the Lord of the harvest (the glorified Christ) was going to send more labourers to different parts of the world to harvest souls for His kingdom without our prayers, the incarnate Jesus would not have told us to pray for it. You must understand that God executes His will and plans on earth primarily through partnerships with His faithful disciples and willing vessels, a privilege that God ultimately rewards.

Sometimes too, God uses the devil and the wicked to execute His will on earth, so that He might demonstrate the superiority of His wisdom over the earthly wisdom of men and craftiness of the devil. That is why the Bible says that, if the principalities of darkness had understood the wisdom of God, they would not have crucified the Lord of glory (*1 Corinthians 2:8*). And concerning human wisdom, the Bible says that "the foolishness of God [is not foolishness at all and] is wiser than men [far beyond human comprehension], and the weakness of God is stronger than men [far beyond the limits of human effort]" (*1 Corinthians 1:25, AMP*).

(vi) ***Praying for your personal wholeness—spirit, soul and body:*** God is concerned with your total wellbeing, your personal wholeness; this was the assurance that the Apostle Paul gave to the church in Thessalonica. He wrote to them, saying:

> Now may the God of peace himself sanctify you wholly, and may your whole spirit and soul and body be kept blameless at the coming of our Lord Jesus Christ. He who calls you is faithful, and he will do it.
>
> *1 Thessalonians 5:23-24, RSV*

There are three dimensions of personal wholeness: healing, sanctification, and deliverance from all demonic operations. If anyone is completely sanctified and kept blameless in his spirit, soul and body until the coming of the Lord Jesus Christ or the end of his life on earth, it means that he is totally free from every form of bodily infirmity, depression or demonic attacks on the soul, as well as contamination or defilement of the spirit.

Bodily wholeness includes effective functionality of every organ or part of the body, as God in His goodness intended it. That is why God is not only committed in His Word to healing sicknesses but also to performing recreative and restorative miracles, such as healing the lame, the blind, the deaf, the dumb, and the barren. Do these problems exist today among God's children? Yes, they do, but God is committed to solving them, as He did in biblical times and still does in our day. *Exodus 23:26* provides that there shall be no barrenness or sterility among God's people, and none shall suffer miscarriage in pregnancy. Safe childbearing is God's will, and He has also instituted marriage as His authorized way for women to bear children.[13]

Some Christians—out of an inadequate understanding of God's Word, His love, and His goodness—entertain doubts as to whether it is God's will to heal them when they are sick or to deliver them when they are buffeted and attacked by demons. By the grace of God, I have prayed for a number of sick and demon-afflicted pastors (and other children of God) poisoned by this type of spiritual ignorance, and the Lord set them free.

Most of those pastors had erroneously believed that, because they were serving the Lord and diverse miracles were happening through them, their own prayers for healing and deliverance from demonic oppression would be instantly answered. But then they were sometimes sick and heavily oppressed by demons for many years, and their prolonged fasting and prayers did not set them free. Some became frustrated and angry with God for "forsaking" them, an unscriptural belief that complicated their problems. What they lacked was appropriate knowledge, but God has always shown mercy to His children (pastors included) when they are properly counselled and prayed for.

God wants us to prosper and be in sound health, and He wants our souls to likewise prosper. Hence, everyone who came to Jesus asking in faith for healing or deliverance from demonic oppression received it. *Isaiah 53:4-5* says that Jesus Himself took our infirmities and bore our sicknesses in His body when He was crucified on the cross of Calvary, and by His stripes we are healed.

Praying for healing is a faith enforcement action to claim and maintain that which Jesus accomplished for us over 2000 years ago.

Although God can heal supernaturally, He does also heal by natural means, using doctors and medical intervention. Many Christians erroneously believe that supernatural or miraculous healing comes from God, but healing by medical science is not of God. The question is, if healing by medical science is not of God, then where is it from? Men or demons? The visible things we see were not made by things that are visible but from the unseen world. Apostle James assures us that "Every good gift and every perfect gift is from above, and comes down from the Father of lights, with whom there is no variation or shadow of turning" (*James 1:17*). Healing through medical science is a good gift; the technical knowledge and skills behind it are from the heavenly Father, the Father of lights.

Many years ago, a woman approached me in Bradford for prayer, ahead of her medical appointment to remove kidney stones from her body. I prayed for God to heal her supernaturally without surgery; she said amen to that and walked away. I had previously prayed in a similar manner for several other people prior to their surgical appointments, and God had healed them, leading to the cancelations of those proposed surgeries. About three weeks later, I saw the same woman and inquired about her health. She looked much healthier than the last time I met her. With some apparent sense of apprehension, she told me she had gone for the surgery and had felt better afterwards.

I cheerfully replied, "Praise God the surgery was successful," and she was taken aback by my warm response. Then she more confidently added that the symptoms had persisted after my prayers, and she didn't want to contact me again before going for the surgery because I would think that she didn't have faith.

I quickly corrected her, saying that God also heals through medical science and that it takes faith in God and in His mercy to have a successful surgery. I reminded her of the scripture that says, "*Is there* no balm in Gilead, *Is there* no physician there?

Why then is there no recovery for the health of the daughter of my people?" (*Jeremiah 8:22*). We know well enough that the apostle who wrote the book of Luke was a physician who worked for the advancement of the gospel of Christ.

Nowadays, when people contact me for prayers ahead of an impending medical surgery, I will first ask them what they want the Lord to do for them, and then take it from there. Sometimes, it is easier for people to have faith in a successful surgery than in supernatural healing, especially in a country like the United Kingdom, where practically all medical treatment is free under the National Health Service.

(vii) **Laying up treasures in heaven**: The Lord commanded His followers to work for and accumulate treasures in heaven, not on earth:

> Do not lay up for yourselves treasures on earth, where moth and rust destroy and where thieves break in and steal; but lay up for yourselves treasures in heaven, where neither moth nor rust destroys and where thieves do not break in and steal. For where your treasure is, there your heart will be also.
>
> *Matthew 6:19-21*

The various works we do wholeheartedly and passionately for the advancement of the kingdom of God, including the money we give, are all part of heavenly treasures that attract rewards from the Lord, both in this life and throughout eternity. Laying up heavenly treasures—as opposed to earthly wealth—is against the natural order of life and requires living a life of daily sacrifice, so that you can be a blessing to God and mankind.

Today, many Pentecostal or charismatic Christians have been wrongly taught to believe that our personal prosperity is everything. Our prosperity *is* important to God, and it is a major promise of the scriptures, but we must be wary of the distorted versions of the prosperity gospel preached by many who take advantage of others for self-aggrandizement. As I have already pointed out, God's blessings are meant for us to be a channel of blessing to others, and you don't wait until you have everything, with some surplus, before you can start to bless others. We are commanded to be a blessing to others *as we have opportunity*, beginning from or especially to those of the household of faith. Christians are also encouraged in the New Testament to lay down their lives for the brethren as a sign of love, just as Jesus laid down His life for us.

When we pray and act on the grace of sharing our material possessions with the brethren, we are praying and doing the will of God. You can make it a personal obligation to bless somebody periodically (for example, monthly) with something substantial and sacrificial. The Bible tells the story of how Jesus offered a rich young man an opportunity to lay up treasures in heaven, but the man did not take it up because his heart was tied too much to his earthly possessions:

> Now behold, one came and said to Him, "Good Teacher, what good thing shall I do that I may have eternal life?"
>
> So He said to him, "Why do you call Me good? No one *is* good but One, *that is,* God. But if you want to enter into life, keep the commandments."
>
> He said to Him, "Which ones?"
>
> Jesus said, "'You shall not murder,' 'You shall not commit adultery,' 'You shall not steal,' 'You shall not bear false witness,' 'Honor your father and *your* mother,' and, 'You shall love your neighbor as yourself.'"
>
> The young man said to Him, "All these things I have kept from my youth. What do I still lack?"
>
> **Jesus said to him, "If you want to be perfect, go, sell what you have and give to the poor, and you will have treasure in heaven; and come, follow Me."**
>
> But when the young man heard that saying, he went away sorrowful, for he had great possessions.
>
> *Matthew 19:16-22*

Funnily enough, this rich man claimed that, from his youth, he had kept all the commandments of God which Jesus enumerated, including the commandment to love your neighbour as yourself. But when Jesus tested him on a practical dimension of loving your neighbour — "sell what you have and give to the poor, and you will have treasure in heaven" — he failed miserably.

In fact, the Lord wanted him to use his treasures on earth to secure for himself treasures in heaven, but the rich man was not interested in having treasures in heaven. He wanted only his treasures on earth. May the Lord give every one of us the grace to henceforth prioritize having treasures in heaven over treasures on earth. And may you use your God-given wealth to earn treasures in heaven by supporting godly causes and agendas, In Jesus' Name.

It was on account of the obstinacy of this rich man that Jesus made that famous declaration which some have taken out of context, that it is easier for a camel to go through the eye of a needle than for a rich man to enter the kingdom of God (*Matthew 19:24*). Having wealth can potentially hinder many people from accepting Christ, entering the kingdom of God, and serving the Lord diligently. The enemy is behind this. But Apostle Paul tells us how the rich can enter the kingdom of heaven—by using their riches to do good in practical ways, thereby laying up treasures for eternal life:

> As for the rich in this present world, instruct them not to be conceited *and* arrogant, nor to set their hope on the uncertainty of riches, but on God, who richly *and* ceaselessly provides us with everything for our enjoyment.
>
> **Instruct them to do good, to be rich in good works, to be generous, willing to share [with others]. In this way storing up for themselves the *enduring* riches of a good foundation for the future, so that they may take hold of that which is truly life.**
>
> *1 Timothy 6:17-19, AMP*

(viii) ***Praying according to rhema or a heavenly vision***: This implies praying according to the spoken or prophetically revealed will and plan of God for you, your family, church, community or nation, or anything else inspired by the Spirit of God. Every rhema is meant to be a prayer pointer or an instruction to guide your actions. The rhema could be one directly received by you or by a trusted servant of God to whom you are connected. It could also be in the form of genuine prophetic utterances made concerning you, the type with which Apostle Paul exhorted his spiritual son Timothy—that, inspired by previous prophecies spoken about him, he should wage the good warfare, holding on to faith and a good conscience (*1 Timothy 1:18-19*).

Another example is the prophetic letter (a rhema from the Lord) that Jeremiah sent to the elders, priests, and prophets of Judah whom King Nebuchadnezzar had carried into captivity in Babylon. The letter foretold that their deportation would last for seventy years, after which the Lord would bring them back to their homeland (*Jeremiah 29:1-10*). About seventy years later, Daniel (who was one of the exiles) read Jeremiah's prophecy and sought the Lord in prayer, supplication and fasting, requesting that He should end the desolation of Jerusalem and the captivity of the people (*Daniel 9:1-27*). The Lord granted Daniel's supplication and even went beyond answering his prayers for the restoration of Jerusalem to give him prophetic visions about the coming of the Messiah and the end-time anti-Christ.

God speaks to us in various ways. Your own personal rhema includes the dreams and visions that God has given you. Stay on them and make each of them a prayer point. If they are positive revelations, pray for God to hasten their manifestation in due season and block every opposition from the devil. The story is told in *Genesis 37:39-50*, of how Joseph received revelations about God's destiny for him through dreams which took at least 13 years before coming to fruition. Over the long years that he waited, the word of the Lord tested him (*Psalm 105:19*), and God used the tribulations he passed through to prune and prepare him for the challenges ahead.

If your personal rhema are negative revelations about what the adversary has done or is planning to do, you have to counteract them and resist the evil powers behind them. If the rhema are warnings or instructions from God concerning your intentions and actions, then you need to ask God for the grace and wisdom to amend your ways and submit to His divine counsel and direction. It is important that you write down your own rhema to guide you in prayer and supplication.

(ix) **Doing good at all costs**: Believers are saved, justified, and equipped with the Holy Spirit and the Word of God, so that they can do what is pleasing to God—for example, by "doing good" to others. Jesus has already set us an example by always doing good and, from God's perspective, no unrighteousness was found in Him. Jesus passionately did good, not counting the cost; and doing good for humanity, according to God's will, cost Him His life. Similarly, it is the will of God that, by doing good, believers may put to silence the ignorance of foolish men; for it is better, if it is the will of God [*and sometimes it could be*], to suffer for doing good than for doing evil (*1 Peter 2:15; 3:17*).

(x) **Interceding for others**: Interceding for others in prayer, just as Jesus interceded for us during His earthly ministry (and ever lives in glory to always make intercession for us), is in the perfect will of God. We can also intercede for nations, cities and communities, for strangers, and for people in positions of governmental authority. Indeed, the Bible exhorts us to intercede for all people. Apostle Paul stressed this point in his first letter to Timothy:

> Therefore, I exhort first of all that supplications, prayers, intercessions, *and* giving of thanks be made for all men, for kings and all who are in authority, that we may lead a quiet and peaceable life in all godliness and reverence. For this *is* good and acceptable in the sight of God our Savior, who desires all men to be saved and to come to the knowledge of the truth.
>
> *1 Timothy 2:1-4*

(xi) ***Giving thanks to God in all things***: Giving thanks in prayer in all things is God's will for every one of His children—in health and in sickness, in fortunes and in misfortunes, in victory and in defeat, in success and in failure, in progress and in setbacks, in receiving the desired answers to our prayers and in our prayers not being answered, and so forth. Whenever undesirable things happen and we still have life, it is important to remember that it could have been worse; that it is by His mercies that we are not consumed; that the sufferings we go through in this life are no more than what our brethren throughout the world are also experiencing; and that many who have run this Christian race before us and prevailed have passed through worse tribulations.

The Bible admonishes Christians to "rejoice always, pray without ceasing, in everything give thanks; for this is the will of God in Christ Jesus for you" (*1 Thessalonians 5:16-18*). The will of God for us in Christ Jesus is not necessarily the bad things that occasionally happen to us, because God is not behind most bad things that happen to us. But giving thanks to Him in all circumstances is in His perfect will for us.

Generally, most things that believers ask God for, in the course of their daily lives, are scripturally in line with His will. But many do not realize this, which often causes their prayers to be adulterated with doubt, impatience, a wrong attitude, carelessness, or double-mindedness. God has "blessed us with all spiritual blessings in heavenly *places* in Christ" (*Ephesians 1:3, KJV*). When we know from scripture that what we are asking God to do in prayer is in line with His will, we must avoid a doubting and beggarly mentality. Instead, we must approach the throne of grace with the confidence that God is willing and abundantly able to grant our petitions.

Box 3.1: Pause to actively pray these prayer pointers

1) Lord, may you give me the spirit of wisdom and revelation of the knowledge of your will, IJN.

2) My heavenly Father, help me to truly repent of all evil works and besetting sins that hinder my relationship with you, IJN.

3) My heavenly Father, sanctify me by the precious Blood of Jesus and give me the grace to grow in sanctification and in the fear of God, IJN.

4) Lord, help me to henceforth be more passionate in my endeavours for the advancement of your kingdom, IJN.

5) Lord, help me to henceforth make deliberate plans and efforts to preach your gospel to others and win souls for your heavenly kingdom, IJN.

6) Lord, help me to henceforth prioritize my prayers for the advancement of your kingdom and the establishment of your will here on earth, IJN.

7) By the power of the Holy Spirit, I decree that every positive revelation I have received from the Lord shall be established at its appointed time, IJN.

8) I command every veil of darkness covering my spiritual eyes to be destroyed by fire, IJN.

9) I break the stranglehold of the evil one who is thwarting the salvation and deliverance of my loved ones, IJN (you could specify the names of those you are interceding for).

10) Lord, may you release upon me the power to constantly walk in divine revelation through godly dreams and visions, IJN.

11) My heavenly Father, establish me in every spiritual gift that will help me to fulfil my destiny and the ministry that I have received from the Lord, IJN.

12) Lord, I thank you for answering my prayers now and always, In Jesus' Name.

Chapter 4

Our Lord's Prayer and Beyond

Jesus' disciples once asked Him to teach them how to pray as John the Baptist taught his disciples. Without hesitation, Jesus taught them to pray, implying that we need to learn how to pray, improve on how we pray, and teach others too. What is popularly known as "Our Lord's Prayer"—which contains Jesus' exact words as recorded in the Bible—is the prayer pattern that Jesus taught His disciples. What Jesus taught them is a template, not necessarily a prayer to be chanted by rote, even though there is certainly no reason why we cannot pray it regularly with heartfelt passion and faith.

The Bible says that we do not know how to pray as we ought to, but the Holy Spirit helps us in our weaknesses, guiding us to pray according to the mind and will of God (*Romans 8:26*). Hence, an important ministry of the Holy Spirit is that of quickening and helping the children of God to pray according to God's will.

We can use Our Lord's Prayer as a guide to learning how to improve our prayer life, supporting each prayer pointer it offers with many relevant scriptures. From Our Lord's Prayer, we can derive at least seven diverse types of prayer:

"In this manner, therefore, pray: **Our Father in heaven, hallowed be Your name.**" [***(i) Prayer of reverence, honour and adoration.***]

"**Your kingdom come. Your will be done on earth as** *it is* **in heaven.**" [***(ii) Prayer for the advancement of God's kingdom —the church—and for God's will to be done in your life, family, community, country, and the world; personally surrendering to God's known will.***]

"**Give us this day our daily bread.**" [***(iii) Prayer for your livelihood and for unbroken supply.***]

"**And forgive us our debts, as we forgive our debtors.**" [***(iv) Prayer for God's forgiveness and mercy through repentance.***]

"And do not lead us into temptation," [*(v) Prayer for vigilance and grace to avoid every temptation and to overcome any tempter who happens to come*].[14]

"But deliver us from the evil one." [*(vii) Prayer for protection from evil and for dominion over the evil one.*]

"For Yours is the kingdom and the power and the glory forever. Amen." [*(vii) Prayerful acknowledgment of God's eternal sovereignty, omnipotence and splendour.*]

Matthew 6:9-13

Based on the pattern that Jesus taught and other relevant Bible passages, prayer can be further broken down into the following major types, which are not mutually exclusive; the list is certainly not exhaustive.

Major Types of Prayers

There are various types of prayers for different purposes. Christians need the wisdom and help of the Holy Spirit to pray the prayers that could yield effective results in their specific circumstances. Praying the wrong prayer could unnecessarily delay the desired outcome, prolong an undesirable condition, and perhaps result in frustration.

Many types of prayers have been identified by leading Bible teachers. Kenneth E. Hagin (2007:7-8), for example, has summarized the nine different types of prayers in the Bible as follows:

(i) **The Prayer of Faith**: the prayer of petition that changes things (*Matthew 21:22; Mark 11:24*). This prayer, always to be based on God's revealed will in His Word, never contains an "if".

(ii) **The Prayer of Consecration**: the prayer of consecration and dedication of our lives for God's use—to go anywhere and do anything. In this prayer, we pray, "If it be Thy will" (*Luke 22:42*).

(iii) **The Prayer of Commitment**: casting your cares upon the Lord in prayer (*1 Peter 5:7*).

(iv) **The Prayer of Worship**: (*Luke 24:52; Acts 13:1-4*).

(v) **The Prayer of Agreement**: (*Matthew 18:18-20*).

(vi) *Prayer in the Spirit:* praying in tongues (*1 Corinthians 14:14-15*).

(vii) *United Prayer*: (*Acts 4:23-31*).

(viii) *The Prayer of Supplication*.

(ix) *Intercessory Prayers*.

Hagin's ninefold classification, combined with the seven types of prayers derived from Our Lord's Prayer above, are an illuminating starting point to aid in our understanding of the various dimensions and purposes of prayer. And now, let me throw more light on the different types of prayers identifiable in the Holy Scriptures:

(1) Prayer of worship, reverence and adoration

We worship and reverence God for who He is—a perfect, merciful and loving Eternal Father. Jesus gave us a good example of this, when He started His prayer with worship: "Our Father, who art in heaven, hallowed by your name." *Genesis 24:23-27* gives us another example, where we see Abraham's servant worshipping the Lord for leading him to the house of his master's brethren. He worshipped God for the good things that were happening to him. In *Job 1:18-21*, we have yet another example, this time of Job worshipping the Lord when things were going badly for him, after Satan had attacked him and he had lost all his children and possessions. We are to prayerfully worship the Lord in both good and bad times.

(2) Prayer of repentance and forgiveness of sin

Our Lord's Prayer leads us to ask God to "forgive us our trespasses, as we forgive those who trespass against us". An instructive example of this can be found in *1 Kings 21:1-29*, which tells the story of Ahab and Jezebel. God pronounced judgment on these two evil rulers of Israel for killing Naboth and taking his vineyard. On hearing the judgment, the wicked King Ahab repented of his sin immediately (but without any restitution to his victims), humbling himself through fasting, and God forgave him. Queen Jezebel, on the other hand, remained adamant, refusing to repent. God's judgment was later executed against her (see *2 Kings 9:30-37*).

(3) Prayer of thanksgiving and praise

God wants thanksgiving and praise to be our lifestyle. We praise God by recounting His goodness and mercies. The Bible tells us to "pray without ceasing, in everything give thanks; for this is the will of God in Christ Jesus for you" (*1 Thessalonians 5:17-18*); and (as recounted earlier) *Philippians 4:6* also exhorts us, "Do not be anxious about anything, but in everything by prayer and supplication with thanksgiving let your requests be made known to God."

(i) Thanksgiving is required before a miracle, as often as we pray for one (*John 11:40-44*).

(ii) Thanksgiving is required when we receive a miracle (*Luke 17:11-19*).

(iii) Thanksgiving is required when God fails to do a miracle we have expected or prayed for (*Daniel 6:6-10*).

(iv) Praise, like worship, is required of us at all times, both in good and bad times (*Psalm 34:1-8*).

(4) Prayer of petition

This is "the asking and receiving prayer" which Jesus espoused in *Luke 11:9-13*. It works in a similar manner to when a petitioner argues his case in a court of law. In a prayer of petition, you are required to bring your strong reasons to argue your case before the throne of grace, Jesus being your Advocate before the Father (*Isaiah 41:21; 43:26; Romans 8:34*). It is in Jesus' name and by His merit that we confidently approach God's throne.

Jabez was living a life of extreme pain and poverty when he prayed a prayer of petition, and he received all that he asked for:

> And Jabez called on the God of Israel saying, "Oh, that You would bless me indeed, and enlarge my territory, that Your hand would be with me, and that You would keep *me* from evil, that I may not cause pain!" So, God granted him what he requested.
>
> *1 Chronicles 4:10*

Bruce Wilkinson, founder and president of Teach Every Nation (TEN) ministries has run a highly successful global outreach, teaching the prayer of Jabez and impacting the lives of tens of thousands of people.

His little book, published in 2000 and titled *The Prayer of Jabez*, is a Number One *New York Times* bestseller. Wilkinson essentially challenges his audiences and readers to make a bold, unique petition to God, which I could paraphrase as follows:

> *So, why not ask God to bless you as Jabez did? Ask God to enlarge your territory, to give you more opportunities to make a mark for Him. Don't focus or dwell on your limitations and weaknesses, but trust in the power of God, with whom all things are possible. Ask God to lay His mighty hand on you; pray as Jabez prayed: "Let your hand be with me." God's hand upon you makes all the difference you need; it is the touch of greatness.*
>
> *Ask God to keep you from evil and the evil one; to also help you overcome and avoid every temptation to sin against Him. Watch your desires prayerfully so that they do not lead you into temptation and sin.*

(5) Prayer of supplication and importunity

Jesus taught that, in our prayers of petition, we should pray with importunity, persisting until we receive what we asked for:

> And he [Jesus] said unto them, Which of you shall have a friend, and shall go unto him at midnight, and say unto him, Friend, lend me three loaves; For a friend of mine in his journey is come to me, and I have nothing to set before him?
>
> And he from within shall answer and say, Trouble me not: the door is now shut, and my children are with me in bed; I cannot rise and give thee.
>
> I say unto you, Though he will not rise and give him, because he is his friend, yet **because of his importunity** he will rise and give him as many as he needeth.
>
> *Luke 11:5-8, KJV*

Prayers of importunity work better with persistent or even occasional fasting, according to one's capacity to fast. We can add to this, day and night supplications, which Apostle Paul mentioned in his first letter to Timothy (*1 Timothy 5:5*); this is especially effective when we enter into intercession for others, a topic we will examine in the next section.

(6) Intercessory prayer

To intercede is to stand in the gap in prayer for another or for a land or people. It is a continuous type of selfless prayer and works best with occasional or regular fasting. Sin creates a gap between God and man, and a righteous intercessor stands in that gap, praying to invoke mercy and avert God's judgment:

> First of all, then, I urge that supplications, prayers, intercessions, and thanksgivings be made for all men, for kings and all who are in high positions, that we may lead a quiet and peaceable life, godly and respectful in every way.
>
> *1 Timothy 2:1-2, RSV*

Interceding for political leaders, that we might have good governance, is important for spreading the gospel because, in times of war and political upheaval, everybody's life is in danger and spreading the gospel is logistically hindered (Hagin, 1991:9). Six key things are important in intercession:

(i) Intercessory prayer is selfless. It is not about your own personal agenda, but God's divine agenda and will for somebody else. Intercession is praying for the benefit of other people, groups, churches, communities or nations, in line with divine purpose.

(ii) Effective intercession must be target-driven, intense, resilient, and defiant.

(iii) As an intercessor, you should not be discouraged by what the person you are interceding for is doing or not doing because you could be fasting and praying but the person is eating and sinning.

(iv) Intercession requires longsuffering, faith and compassion (*Luke 2:36-38*).

(v) Intercession requires proactively combatting (binding and loosing) the powers of darkness behind that condition, in the name of the Lord Jesus Christ.

(vi) To be effective, intercession must be enabled by the Holy Spirit, who has a major ministry on earth of helping born-again believers in intercession. Praying in the spirit and prayers of self-edification are important ways by which the Holy Spirit can help us in intercessory prayer.

(7) Praying in the spirit

Praying in the spirit, with evidence of speaking in "an unknown tongue"[15], comes through the baptism of the Holy Spirit:

> For he who speaks in a tongue does not speak to men but to God, for no one understands him; however, in the spirit he speaks mysteries… He who speaks in a tongue edifies himself…
>
> *1 Corinthians 14:2, 4*

The Holy Spirit helps our weaknesses in prayer by interceding for us with groanings which cannot be uttered (*Romans 8:26*) in articulate words. The Holy Spirit mostly helps us in intercession when we pray in a spiritual tongue, because He searches the deep things of God (*1 Corinthians 2:10*) and therefore uses our praying in a spiritual tongue to align our prayers with the will of God, especially when we may not know God's will or what exactly to pray.

Furthermore, there are some overly generic prayers we are urged to pray in the scriptures, which we can only effectively pray in tongues with the help of the intercessory ministry of the Holy Spirit. For instance, the Bible teaches that "supplications, prayers, intercessions and thanksgiving should be made for all men," which literally means *all* human beings in the world. Interceding for "all men" makes spiritual sense because the Bible further teaches that "God our Saviour… desires all men to be saved and to come to the knowledge of the truth" (*1 Timothy 2:3-4*).

Generic intercessions of this nature are best done by praying in the spirit and doing it over long intervals. There are some sinners whose only hope of salvation could depend on this type of intercession; the Holy Spirit knows them and would save them as believers intercede for them by actively praying in the spirit. However, specific intercessions on behalf of individuals known to us can also be effectively made by praying in the spirit.

Praying in the spirit is almost always praying that aligns with God's will. When we pray in the spirit, it is our human spirit that prays, but this could grow in tempo and depth into travails and groanings through the quickening power and help of the Holy Spirit.

How does one receive the baptism of the Holy Spirit, which is paramount for praying in the spirit? The commonest way is probably the method used by Apostle Paul when he encountered some new disciples in Ephesus, who only knew about John's baptism (the baptism of repentance) and had never heard of the Holy Spirit or His baptism. Paul taught them the gospel of Jesus Christ, linking it to John's baptism, which they had already received; then, "when Paul had laid hands on them, the Holy Spirit came upon them, and they spoke with tongues and prophesied" (*Acts 19:6*).

I have used this method effectively to pray for many people to receive the baptism of the Holy Spirit, including children as young as eight years old. However, this was not how I myself received the Holy Spirit's baptism in 1994, three years after I was saved. Between 1991 and 1994, I responded to altar calls to receive the baptism of the Holy Spirit in our local fellowship. Each time, hands were laid on me, but I never received it, although a few others always did. It was in the course of my midnight prayers, which had become regular by 1994, that I suddenly burst into a new tongue as I was agonizing in earnest intercession for someone.

Many born-again Christians still do not believe that people in our time can experience the baptism of the Holy Spirit with the evidence of speaking in a spiritual tongue. I have come across several sceptics, especially in Europe. Between 2001 and 2005, I attended a local branch of the Wesley Reformed Church in the UK and, on one occasion when the issue of baptism of the Holy Spirit came up in a bible study class, practically all the members were of the view that the experience only happened (and ended) during the days of the Apostles, as recorded in the book of Acts.

I took a different position and told them that I was baptized in the Holy Spirit and spoke in a spiritual tongue. The church was entirely Caucasian, and I was a lone voice from Sub-Saharan Africa, struggling to convince those elderly and middle-aged Caucasians, some of whom had been born again before I was born, that the Holy Spirit's baptism was still happening in our time. They were totally unpersuaded. The church's foremost elder, who was teaching that Bible class, agreed with the dominant opinion and politely dismissed my claim that I was baptized in the Holy Spirit and that the experience was not confined to the apostolic age. People have many weird and unexplainable spiritual experiences these days, they subtly but firmly concluded.

The pastor of the church, who was sitting in the audience, kept mute throughout the polarized discussion. About two days later, this pastor—an exceptionally amiable and well-informed believer—turned up at my house on a short-notice scheduled visit, as he occasionally did. Recalling the discussion during the bible class, he acknowledged that I was right about the baptism of the Holy Spirit still happening in our day. He said that he was also baptized in the Holy Spirit, like me, but couldn't say it during the bible class because he knew the theological conviction of his congregants. "They would never have believed me," he said helplessly.

(8) Prayer of self-edification

"Anyone who speaks in a tongue edifies themselves," wrote Apostle Paul (*1 Corinthians 14:4, NIV*), implying that praying in a spiritual tongue has the additional advantage of building up our spiritual life and deepening our fellowship and intimacy with God. Since such self-edification is available to "anyone who speaks in a tongue", it follows that, to pray self-edifying prayers, we need to receive the baptism of the Holy Spirit. It is also important for us to stay persistently in the place of prayer for long stretches of time, because this is a type of prayer that could progressively open the door to divine revelations and prophetic insights, especially if combined with periodic fasting.

Since the Holy Spirit can use praying in tongues to align your prayers with God's will, there will be times when, as you continue praying in a tongue for some time, the Holy Spirit could provide some clarity in your spirit about a specific thing or person He wants you to pray for—which could help you to switch back and forth between praying in the spirit and in your understanding, as well as using relevant scriptures to support your prayers.

(9) Prayer of inquiry for divine direction and to surrender oneself to God's known will

A prayer of inquiry is essential when things are inexplicably or mysteriously going wrong, and your prayers do not seem to be achieving the desired impact. It is also necessary when you are at a crossroads or in the valley of indecision, where divine counsel is required for a wise decision, choice or direction. A prayer of inquiry works better with fasting. David prayed it many times and, on each occasion, he received God's counsel and direction. To cite just one example:

> Now there was a famine in the days of David for three years, year after year; and David inquired of the Lord. And the Lord answered, "*It is* because of Saul and *his* bloodthirsty house, because he killed the Gibeonites."
>
> *2 Samuel 21:1*

May the Lord answer you any time you pray a prayer of inquiry, so that neither the adversary nor the wicked can gain any advantage over you, IJN. In the event that you already know God's direction or will in a matter, it is also crucial to prayerfully commit yourself to doing His will and not try to evade it, as Jonah attempted to do by running off—to the displeasure of God—which provoked Him to inflict a chastising ordeal upon the prophet (see *Jonah 1*).

When we already know God's will, we also need prayer to walk in full compliance and not execute His will half-heartedly—as Saul, the first king of Israel, did and thereby incurred the wrath of God (see *1 Samuel 15*).

Jesus knew that it was God's will for Him to suffer unprovoked persecution and death on a cross for the sins of humanity. When the appointed time came, He prayed to surrender and commit Himself to the will of God, famously saying, "Father, if it is Your will, take this cup away from Me; nevertheless, not My will, but Yours, be done" (*Luke 22:42*). Jesus subdued His own will and submitted to the will of the heavenly Father, humbling Himself and becoming "obedient to the point of death, even the death of the cross" (*Philippians 2:8*).

(10) Prayer of authority and command

This kind of prayer enables us to exercise and enforce the authority the Lord has given us over the forces of darkness and to live a life of dominion and victory on earth (*Luke 10:19*; *Matthew 10:1*). This exercising of authority and command was a distinguishing mark of Jesus' ministry, as evidenced by His authority in teaching and over unclean spirits. The people were astonished because He taught as one who had authority and not as the scribes (*Mark 1:22*).

When Jesus rebuked the violent, unclean spirit that had convulsed a man in the Capernaum synagogue, the people exclaimed, "What new doctrine *is* this? For with authority, He commands even the unclean spirits, and they obey Him" (*Mark 1:27*). And when He encountered a similar unclean spirit that was troubling a boy, Jesus rebuked the spirit saying, "You dumb and deaf spirit, I command you, come out of him, and never enter him again" (*Mark 9:25, RSV*)

"All authority has been given to Me in heaven and on earth," declared Jesus after His resurrection, and He has transferred this authority to His disciples to continue all the good works He was sent by the Father to do on earth, charging them to exercise this same authority in His name. As followers of Jesus Christ, we have been mandated to teach, preach, cast out unclean spirits and work miracles with divine authority and power; and the Lord will be with us to back us up as we do His will (*Matthew 28:18-20*).

When praying prayers of authority and command, it is important to keep the following in mind:

(i) Be bold and confident in the Lord. The Bible says the righteous are bold as a lion (*Proverbs 28:1*), and the Lord has given us a spirit of boldness, not a spirit of fear (*2 Timothy 1:7*).

(ii) Do not allow Satan to gain any strongholds in your life: Jesus got fantastic results all the time because the prince of darkness had nothing on Him. If the enemy has strongholds in your life, you risk being embarrassed, like the seven sons of the Jewish chief priest Sceva (see *Acts 19:14-17*). But even without any satanic embarrassment, you are not likely to get the desired results most of the time if Satan has a stronghold in your life.

(iii) Sensitivity to the will of God and the indwelling Holy Spirit is essential: God will only establish the things you decree or command that are in line with His will (*Job 22:28, KJV*)

(iv) Understand when and how to combine prayer with fasting for effective results (*Mark 9:17-29*), as well as when to seek a prayer of agreement with someone else or prayer support from others.

(11) Spiritual warfare prayer

Prayer can be an instrument of spiritual warfare when you use scriptures to deploy pre-emptive and defensive assaults on the adversary, by calling on the God of vengeance to fight your battle against the forces of evil. The Bible says that God is angry with the wicked every day (*Psalm 7:11*), and many of them will not stop their wicked enterprises if they do not see the mighty hand of God. God had to judge the gods of Egypt and the wickedness of Pharaoh for the Israelites to be liberated from over 400 years of bondage in Egypt. God had to judge the wickedness and pride of King Nebuchadnezzar of Babylon by degrading him to the ignoble level of a forest beast for seven years to teach him wisdom.

Box 4.1: Pause to actively pray these prayer pointers

1) My heavenly Father, I give you thanks for your mercies and worthiness, and I reverence your holy name, IJN.
2) My heavenly Father, I thank you for giving us your Son Jesus Christ as an eternal sacrifice for our redemption, IJN.
3) My heavenly Father, I thank you for exalting the name of Jesus above every other name and that, at the name of Jesus, every knee must bow, IJN.
4) Lord, give me the grace to revive my prayer life, spending more time in praying diverse kinds of prayers, IJN.
5) My heavenly Father, help me henceforth to pray more, according to your will and in line with your Word, IJN.
6) Lord, may you show mercy to our political leaders at all levels of government and help them to govern with wisdom, compassion, and the fear of God, IJN.
7) Lord, remove the wicked from positions of power and influence in our country, IJN.
8) My heavenly Father, may you reveal to me great and hidden things that will stop the enemy from taking advantage of me, IJN.
9) By the mercies of the Living God, I surrender every burden of the adversary in my life and lay it all down at the feet of Jesus because He cares for me, IJN.
10) I command every burdensome yoke of the evil one upon my life and destiny to be broken by the power of the Holy Spirit, IJN.
11) God of vengeance, may you vindicate me by fire today against all my adversaries, IJN.
12) I command all stubborn pursuers who dig a pit for me and my family to fall into their own pit, IJN.
13) I command all invisible arrows of the enemy fired against me and my loved ones to go back to their sender, IJN.
14) My heavenly Father, may you reveal to me great and mighty things that will help to advance my destiny, IJN.
15) Lord, I thank you for all your answers to my prayers, IJN.

Individual Prayer Versus Corporate Prayer and God's Responsiveness

There is a place for individual prayer and a place for corporate prayer in the life of every child of God. Both are essential for a healthy and victorious Christian life. It is necessary to spend sufficient time in God's presence on personal prayer, worship, and study of the Word on a day-to-day basis. "He who dwells in the secret place of the Most High," avers the Psalmist about personal devotion, "shall abide under the shadow of the Almighty. I will say of the Lord, *He is* my refuge and my fortress; My God, in Him I will trust" (*Psalm 91:1-2*).

Corporate prayer, on the other hand, is vital because Jesus made a commitment under the new covenant to build His church, the body or community of believers, and the gates of hell shall not prevail against it. Where two or three are gathered in fellowship in His name to pray and worship, the Lord is in their midst to supply all the needed grace. It is easier for Satan's kingdom, which carries out formidable warfare against the children of God, to overcome an isolated lone-ranger Christian than those who are part of a strong, prayerful fellowship.

Satan knows there is strength in numbers and unity is power; that is why his kingdom is not divided against itself. The forces and messengers of darkness do not act or attack alone. When they spot an individual who must be stopped by all means, because of the potential threat he represents, they come in their battalions in the physical and spiritual realms.

To hinder and ultimately arrest and crucify Jesus Christ during His earthly ministry, the kingdom of darkness mobilized and deployed the Pharisees, the Sanhedrin, and their well-armed foot soldiers and mobs. To incapacitate the madman at the tombs of the Gadarenes, the kingdom of darkness deployed a legion of demons to torment him. The multitude of unclean spirits that Jesus expelled from the madman entered a herd of about 2,000 swine that rushed down a steep bank into a lake and were all drowned. This single man was apparently tormented and buffeted by at least 2,000 demons. The kingdom of darkness is not kidding in their determined agenda to ruin, hurt and destroy.

The gathering together of the brethren for fellowship with the Father and the Son, corporate prayers, worship, breaking of bread (or holy communion), teaching of sound doctrine, and encouragement of one another, as the early church practised: all these we are admonished not to neglect (*Hebrews 10:25*)—forming, as they do, an essential part of the Christian race. There are prayers that God in His sovereign will may not answer, and miracles that He may not perform, except in a specific place of congregational fellowship or prayer. Corporate prayer and fellowship also come with sanctifying grace and power:

> But if we walk in the light as He is in the light, we have fellowship with one another, and the blood of Jesus Christ His Son cleanses us from all sin.
>
> *1 John 1:7*

Most significantly, it is in the place of corporate prayer that the church can effectively take up her mantle[16] as the spiritual army of the Lord, and wield the authority, anointing and power thereof, against the human and spiritual forces of darkness. When the church prays in unity according to the will of God, whatever she binds in the earthly realm of her jurisdiction is bound in heaven, and whatever she decrees and allows on earth is confirmed by heaven.

God, in His sovereign will, mercy and judgment, determines when and how to respond to every prayer. Embedded in Jesus' parable of the unjust judge—who for a while disregarded the petition of a helpless widow for justice against her wicked adversary, until the judge was wearied by her importunity— is a validation of the elect's prayers for divine justice. The parable finished with the following approving statement:

> Then the Lord said, "Hear what the unjust judge said. **And shall God not avenge His own elect who cry out day and night to Him, though He bears long with them? I tell you that He will avenge them speedily.**"
>
> *Luke 18:6-8*

Every genuine prayer for divine vindication and justice, prayed persistently with a sincere heart and clean hands, will surely provoke God to action. God is a righteous judge, and it is a righteous thing for Him to recompense with affliction those who afflict His children (*2 Thessalonians 1:6*). *Isaiah 26:9* further assures us that "when Your [God's] judgments are in the earth, the inhabitants of the world will learn righteousness."

> **The soul of the wicked desires evil; his neighbour finds no favour in his eyes. When the scoffer is punished, the simple is made wise… The righteous *God* wisely considers the house of the wicked, overthrowing the wicked for *their* wickedness.**
>
> *Proverbs 21:10-12*

Christians are forbidden by scripture from taking direct vengeance against their enemies, because vengeance belongs to the Lord; but sometimes they have to pray and decree divine retribution on stubborn adversaries who—like the wicked characters in the Bible, such as Pharaoh (in the time of Moses), Nebuchadnezzar, Jezebel, and the "Herods"—are determined to inflict maximum pain and relentless harm on the innocent against God's will.

Proverbs 25:5 tells us there are wicked people who must be removed for the throne of the righteous to be established. God rejected Saul as king over Israel because of his stubborn disobedience to divine command, and He consequently chose and anointed David as king to replace him. But, for probably over eight years, David could not ascend to the throne because the wicked king rejected by God did not only stubbornly refuse to vacate the throne but also set out with relentless determination to eliminate the innocent one that God had chosen to replace him. Until Saul was killed by divine arrangement, David was not going to be established on the throne prepared for him, and his life was also in mortal danger from Saul and his forces of evil.

There are lessons to be learnt from Saul's stubborn resolve to perpetuate evil against Israel and the Lord's anointed. Even though the Bible says that all governing authorities are from God, Saul's story tells us that not all persons occupying the highest seats of government necessarily command God's approval. A wicked man rejected and disapproved by God could perpetuate himself in office or steal the position of power from God's chosen vessel and use political power to do evil in society. Over the extended period that Saul was in power as king of Israel against God's will, there was a brutal revival and spread of evil in the land of Israel. This has happened in our time too, in many parts of the world. And it will take the united, strategic prayers of those that know their God to end such regimes of evil and sieges of darkness in all our lands.

In warfare prayer, it is a righteous thing to, among other things, demand that God vindicate us and execute justice against the wicked, which could sometimes cause them to be caught up in the snares they have set and pits they have dug for the righteous, and their evil plots to fall upon their own heads. Those were part of the prayers of Nehemiah and David, and there is scriptural backing for them: see *Nehemiah 4:4; 13:2; Psalm 9:15-16; Proverbs 26:27; Esther 7:10.* You can also pray to disarm the enemy and the wicked spirits behind them, confuse them and frustrate their plans, as well as to thwart their craftiness, so that their hands cannot carry out their wicked enterprises. All these lines of prayer are derived from the Bible.

In general, the commitment of Christians to a lifestyle of prayer is a divine command that should not be contingent on God's responsiveness and the answers we obtain or fail to obtain. However, if by the intercessory ministry and help of the Holy Spirit, we persistently pray in line with God's will, we can be sure that God does hear us, and by faith we can also know that we have received the answers to our prayers. In certain petitions, there could be a time lag between when our prayer is answered by God and the time the expected outcome is manifested or delivered. During the waiting interval, we need to exercise patience and faith, striving to do good and persevering in thanksgiving, fellowship, and praying diverse kinds of prayers.

As we commit ourselves to a lifestyle of persevering prayer, our prayer walk with God will mature and deepen. Stormie Omartian (2005:19-20), bestselling author of *The Power of Praying* series, gives us the following pointers (which I have paraphrased) by which we can know if our prayer walk with God is growing deeper or not.

In a nutshell, our walk with God is still shallow if we love God only because of what He can do for us, pray to Him only when we want something from Him, get angry with Him when He doesn't do as we ask, praise Him only when we get what we want, or try to twist His arm to get Him to do what we want. On the other hand, our walk with God is growing deeper if our prayers reflect that we love Him for *who* He is and not what we can get out of Him: for example, if we start asking Him what *we* can do for *Him*, not just what He can do for us; pray to Him out of a sincere love for being in His presence; praise Him even when life is hard and He doesn't do as we ask; and persevere in our prayers because we believe that He *wants* to give us what we ask for, but preferably according to His good and perfect will.

Box 4.2: Pause to actively pray these prayer pointers

1) My heavenly Father, help me to desire dwelling in your presence through: i) the power of prayer, praying multiple times in a day; ii) the power of your Word, committing myself to reading and studying your Word daily; iii) the power of scripture meditation, reading and meditating on specific verses of your Word daily; iv) the power of corporate fellowship, not neglecting the assembling together of the brethren in fellowship and Christian worship, IJN.

2) Lord, by your divine power, I resist every temptation to dwell on my problems or be anxious about things I cannot humanly handle; I cast down all negative imaginations and take all contrary thoughts in my mind captive to the obedience of Christ, IJN.

3) By the power of the indwelling Holy Spirit, I shall henceforth meditate only on the Word of God and find solutions to my problems in His Word, IJN.

4) My heavenly Father, help me to develop a disciplined and strong prayer life that is anchored in the love of God, IJN.

5) Lord, I tap into your manifold grace to be a daily practitioner of your Word that I hear and study regularly, IJN.

6) Lord, may you help me to grow continuously in the ability to understand your Word and to always discern and reject every wind of erroneous doctrine, IJN.

7) By faith, I receive the grace to begin to practise today everything I have prayed for, and to sustain this practice, IJN.

PART 2

PREVAILING IN THE BATTLES OF LIFE BY YOUR OWN FAITH

Chapter 5

Understanding and Fighting the Battles of Life

Every child of God is saved to become a spiritual soldier of Christ, and every soldier is trained for battle. As soldiers, we are trained not only to fight wars but also to endure stress and hardship on the battlefield, so that we might win. Apostle Paul reminded his spiritual son Timothy of this important dimension of our spiritual calling:

> **You therefore must endure hardship as a good soldier of Jesus Christ.** No one engaged in warfare entangles himself with the affairs of *this* life, that he may please him who enlisted him as a soldier.
>
> *2 Timothy 2:3-4*

In his preceding epistle, Paul had instructed and urged Timothy to "**fight the good fight of faith**" so that he might "lay hold on eternal life," to which he was also called and had made "the good confession in the presence of many witnesses" (*1 Timothy 6:12*).

We too are called to fight the good fight of faith. It *is* a good fight, and the end of it is eternal life and rewards in heaven, to which we are called. Bishop David Oyedepo, one of the greatest biblical faith preachers and authors in modern history, teaches that "the fight of faith" is called the "good fight" because "faith *in the word of God* determines the end from the beginning," "it is both your offensive and defensive weapon," and "the victory is sure."[17]

There are several important dimensions of this good fight of faith. The fight to establish your destiny and fulfil your purpose in life, against all odds, is a good fight of faith. The fight to overcome and live above any besetting sin is a good fight of faith. The fight to fulfil any heavenly vision you carry (that is, a vision received from the Lord) is a good fight of faith. The fight to advance the kingdom of God and have His will established here on earth, as it is in heaven, is a good fight of faith. The fight to be in health above all things and to prosper, even as your soul prospers, is a good fight of faith. The fight to "have life" and "have it more abundantly" (*John 10:10*) is a good fight of faith. The fight to prevent Satan and all unclean spirits from gaining any advantage over you is a good fight of faith.

The good fight is fought in the place of prayer (with fasting) and by the application of the Word of God through faith. Without faith in God and in the power of His Word, you cannot fight the good fight. The good fight is a spiritual fight, which we fight with the help of the Holy Spirit. **The good fight of faith is the fight of *every* believer; the opponent in this fight is the kingdom of darkness**— the devil and unclean spirits, but too often they fight us through our flesh (our natural weaknesses, desires and lustful tendencies). They also fight us through human beings, especially the human members of their kingdom, as well as all others who may yield themselves as useful instruments in their adversarial hands.

The devil and his angels unremittingly execute, ***with ferocious determination***, the fight they have declared against the church and the whole of humanity; but large sections of the church of Jesus Christ—the only organization on earth spiritually equipped to win the battle—seem practically ignorant and carefree about this fight of faith. Commissioning the redeemed to fight the good fight of faith on earth, Jesus declared:

> From the days of John the Baptist until now the kingdom of heaven suffers violent assault, and violent men seize it by force [as a precious prize].
>
> *Matthew 11:12, AMP*

Fighting and winning the good scriptural fight is what we take with us to heaven—that you might "lay hold on eternal life, to which you were also called" (*1 Timothy 6:12*). The crowns and rewards we receive in heaven are an outcome of the good fight of faith. As the glorified Christ declared to the church at Philadelphia, "Hold tight to what you have, so that no one will take your crown [by leading you to renounce the faith]" (*Revelation 3:11, AMP*).

The opposite of the good fight of faith is the bad fight of the flesh. The bad fight is fought in the flesh against fellow human beings—your siblings, workmates, spouse, children, family members, employers, church members, fellow believers, etc. The devil is the unseen enemy behind the bad fight, but the fighters hardly recognize this. They end up fighting just the human fronts, unaware of the unseen spiritual forces behind them. The bad fight is supposed to be the unbelievers' fight; but sadly, many Christians are fiercely and persistently involved in it. Fighting the bad fight takes many to hell, because the devil has taken them captive to do his will. Apostle Paul warned the young Timothy about the nature of the fight he must be careful to avoid:

> Flee also youthful lusts; but pursue righteousness, faith, love, peace with those who call on the Lord out of a pure heart. But avoid foolish and ignorant disputes, knowing that they generate strife. And a servant of the Lord must not quarrel but be gentle to all, able to teach, patient, in humility correcting those who are in opposition, if God perhaps will grant them repentance, so that they may know the truth, **and *that* they may come to their senses *and escape* the snare of the devil, having been taken captive by him to *do* his will.**
>
> *2 Timothy 2:22-26*

Everyone in this life is involved in a fight with invisible and sometimes visible forces. Believers fight the good fight and unbelievers fight the bad fight, but many believers also frequently fight the bad fight. Consequently, everybody has their own fight, and many are fighting multiple fights on several fronts at the same time. Everyone must fight their own fight—whether the good scriptural fight or the bad fleshly fight. Others cannot fight your own fight for you. Compassionate people, family members, and the church can support you in fighting your fight (and this is the proper thing to do), but ultimately it is *your* fight, not theirs. Apostle Paul was speaking to Timothy personally when he charged him to fight the good fight of faith and lay hold on eternal life. Nobody can lay hold on eternal life on your behalf. Everyone makes it to heaven according to how they have fought their own good fight of faith.

There is no battle-free life, either for the righteous or the unrighteous. Jesus made the famous declaration, "Sufficient for the day is its own trouble" (*Matthew 6:34*). Many troubles we face from day to day are battles with spiritual dimensions, and these battles come in various shapes and sizes. You don't need to be a sinner to face the troubles, tribulations and battles of life; they come to all and sundry. However, the major advantage of the redeemed in Christ is that they potentially have more grace to overcome these trials and storms of life—but only on the condition that they walk in the knowledge, wisdom and fear of God, and in faith in Him.

In the narrative that follows, I wish to discuss five important factors that might determine, influence and shape the nature and scale of battles one may fight in life.

(1) Parental and family background

You don't get to choose who your parents are, but you might have many battles to fight in life just because of *who* they are: the good or evil they have done, who hates and fights with them, the circumstances in which you were conceived and born, the blessings or curses you have inherited from your parents, the evil (or righteous) covenants you have inherited from your parental background, and so forth. Spiritually, some people are already extremely disadvantaged from the moment of their birth—dedicated and covenanted to satanic altars, religious cults and unclean spirits by their parents as soon as they were born, and then raised in a spiritual atmosphere of fetish practices and utter darkness. This kind of foundation often shapes the nature of the battles they will have to fight, growing up, and even when they ultimately get saved.

I read with great empathy the story of God's servant and renowned evangelist John Ramirez, who used to be an arch satanic warlock for about 25 years. He recounted in his book (Ramirez, 2021:39-41) the story of his family's experience in serving the kingdom of darkness, and how he passed on to his daughter the same yoke of satanic bondage which he had inherited from his father, who was himself a warlock. It is a chilling story of three generations of a family whose destinies Satan wasted or came close to wasting, as they dutifully served him through diverse diabolical exploits—and, in turn, reaping deeply broken and hopeless lives. The story could have ended badly for John Ramirez too, but for the gracious intervention of the Lord.

In the course of ministering deliverance to many, I have encountered clients with narratives of wasted destinies like those of Ramirez's family, all because of parental initiation into mermaid cults, fetish religions, and witchcraft covens. Some of the lengthiest deliverances I have handled are those connected with families generationally covenanted and dedicated to the service of Satan, which bequeaths to the later generations a perverted heritage and lifestyle characterized by multiple afflictions and struggles, grinding poverty, recurrent or persistent infirmities, failed or truncated basic education, forced or early initiation into sexual immorality, and wasted years spent on satanic assignments. When these clients are going through deliverance, Satan always fights back, unwilling to let them go, thereby prolonging the duration of their struggles to be set free from inherited and acquired satanic yokes and curses. Without a doubt, the family you come from affects the nature of the battles you will face in life.

There are families you could come from, where you will not have to fight extreme poverty from the day you are born until the day you die. You will still have your own fights and battles in life, but poverty will not be one of them. Everybody would like to bequeath this type of family foundation to their children. *Proverbs 13:22* says that a good man leaves an inheritance to his children's children. For some other people, poverty could be their "Number One" constraint, the battle they have to fight from birth, because of who their parents are. Many in various parts of the world, especially in poor, developing countries, have failed to overcome the overwhelming challenges they face in their battle for survival. Hence, the disproportionately high levels of extreme poverty and infant mortality in many developing countries.[18]

There are families you could come from, where building a strong relationship with God will potentially be easier because of who your parents are and the righteous foundation they have laid for you from birth. God testified concerning Abraham, that He knew him, that he would command his children and household after him to keep the way of the Lord and do righteousness and justice (*Genesis 18:19*).

The Psalmist wrote that the descendants of the man who fears the Lord and delights greatly in His commandments will be mighty and blessed on earth (*Psalm 112:1-3*). My biological children have not had to struggle to know the truth of God's Word as much as I struggled, growing up, because of the grace I have acquired in redemption to lay a godly foundation for them from day one. And my own parents have had to struggle even far more than I ever did to know the truth.

There are families you could come from, where all that you inherit spiritually would be a foundation of evil and wickedness which potentially destines you to hell, unless God shows you extraordinary mercy by getting you to see the light of the gospel, believe it and make a U-turn. That was why, when Israel was divided into the northern and southern kingdoms, the northern kingdom produced comparatively more wicked kings (until the extremely evil reign of Menasseh, king of the southern kingdom of Judah, whose abominable atrocities provoked divine judgment against Judah). The northern kingdom of Israel produced comparatively more wicked kings because of the extremely evil foundation established by their first king Jeroboam, a foundation that was generationally reproduced and perpetuated through the ungodly children of the kings who replaced their fathers on the throne.

Over the next 200 years, Jeroboam, the harbinger of ungodly rule in the northern kingdom of Israel, and Ahab, an exceptionally wicked king who emerged later in the line of succession, became the referent standard of wickedness in Israel. All the subsequent evil rulers were said to have walked in the ways of their father Jeroboam or Ahab. Among the many records of this in the Bible, it suffices to give just this example, which recounts the ungodly rule of Ahab's son Ahaziah, king over the northern kingdom of Israel after his father's demise:

> Ahaziah the son of Ahab became king over Israel in Samaria… **He did evil in the sight of the Lord and walked in the [idolatrous] way of his father [Ahab] and of his mother [Jezebel], and in the way of Jeroboam the son of Nebat, who made Israel sin.** He served Baal and worshiped him, **and he provoked the Lord God of Israel to anger, in accordance with everything that his father [Ahab] had done.**
>
> *1 Kings 22:51-53, AMP*

During the time of the prophet Ezekiel, the descendants of Israel—who had inherited the Promised Land from their forefathers—provoked God to anger because they had embraced the wicked ways and ungodly behaviour of the heathen tribes with whom they were cohabiting in the land, and they had also passed on those ungodly normative systems to their descendants. We can read for ourselves, in *Ezekiel 16:44-47*, God's rebuke and condemnation of Israel for imbibing and perpetuating the wicked traditions of the Hittites, Amorites and other heathen nations in their midst. We can also contrast this evil lineage with the legacy left by David—a man who feared God, ruled righteously, and became the measuring reference of godly rule for all subsequent kings who ruled well, most of whom descended from the southern kingdom of Judah and are traceable to King David.

The Bible reveals in *Psalm 112:2* that the descendants of the righteous will be mighty on earth and be blessed but, in *Psalm 37:28*, we see a potential judgment of destruction pronounced on the children of the wicked. Spiritually therefore, the descendants of the righteous and the descendants of the wicked do not start their lives on a level playing field; one has a head-start advantage over the other. This is why it is so important for fathers and mothers to be godly and committed to their parental responsibilities, so that they do not put their children at a disadvantage by bequeathing to them unnecessary spiritual battles that these children will have to fight as they grow up. Even though the grace of God that brings salvation is free and available to all humanity, the chances of getting saved and making it to heaven are brighter if you have Abraham and Sarah as your parents, as opposed to Ahab and Jezebel. Why? Because Abraham is a friend of God and Ahab His enemy.

Does this make God a partial God? Certainly not. The Apostle Peter received a firsthand experience of God's impartiality from the heavenly vision he saw in Acts 10, which was contrary to the tradition held by Peter and his fellow Jews, who hitherto thought that the God of the universe was only interested in the Hebrews. Listen to Peter's rethink: **"In truth I perceive that God shows no partiality. But in every nation, whoever fears Him and works righteousness is accepted by Him"** (*Acts 10:34-35*).

Because of His impartiality, God has made a way of remedy for all those who may have inherited a foundation of ungodliness from their parents. This remedial way is called "repentance" and, in Christ Jesus, the foundational curses of the parents' iniquities can be broken. This is how, according to the prophet Ezekiel, you can avail yourself of God's remedial measures through repentance, if your parents are adamant in committing abominable iniquities:

> But if this sinful man has, in turn, **a son who sees all his father's wickedness, so that he fears God and decides against that kind of life**; he doesn't go up on the mountains to feast before the idols and worship them and does not commit adultery; he is fair to those who borrow from him and doesn't rob them, but feeds the hungry, clothes the needy, helps the poor, does not loan money at interest, and obeys my laws—**he shall not die because of his father's sins; he shall surely live. But his father shall die for his own sins** because he is cruel and robs and does wrong.
>
> *Ezekiel 18: 14-18, TLB*

In my view, the greatest thing that parents can do for their children is to lay a righteous foundation for them in Christ. This is more precious than an inheritance of money, properties or a good education, as important as all these earthly advantages may be. To help lay a godly foundation for their children, it is important for Christian parents to dedicate their children to God in a Bible-believing church, take them to Sunday school and prayer meetings, teach them the Word of God and the fear of God, correct them—using the Word of God—and set them an example of godliness in their own lives. A godly foundation will not only save your children from fighting many unnecessary battles with self-indulgence, immorality and wicked devices, it will also equip them to fight and win the battles of evil pressures and persecution from the children of Belial that they could face in life.

For teenagers and young adults who have the privilege of godly parents, the greatest good you could do for yourself is to continue in the godly foundation your parents have laid for you and resist the perversive pressure to conform to the sinful lifestyle of your peers. You will realize the benefits of doing this as you grow older.

(2) Community background and social identity

I use the term "community background" to broadly capture a person's ancestral community, ethnic community, nationality, religious community, racial community and the likes, because, for so many people, these factors considerably determine their battles in this life. Our social identity oftentimes reflects our community background. We could, as individuals, have multiple identities as a result of overlapping or divergent social identities, which may also have implications for our circumstantial realities and life battles.

In some of the social science theories, such as the Critical Race Theory, this reality about the crosscutting identity-based oppressions that shape inequality in society is called "intersectionality"[19]. For instance, in the United Kingdom a person could be a female, an African immigrant of ethnic Ndebele origin from Zimbabwe, a nurse practitioner and a practising Pentecostal Christian—all at the same time. These various social identities could, in isolation or combination, be the basis for many battles this person will fight in the UK for a greater part of her life. Like parental origin, you do not often choose the community you come from; but in a fallen world, full of bigotries, it can attract or provoke various battles for many people in life.

The irony about community background is that, while it could potentially disadvantage some people, oftentimes—regardless of the just provisions of a country's laws—it could conversely become institutionalized as the basis for diverse undue advantages enjoyed by members of a politically dominant and more privileged community. What is, for instance, called "institutional racism" in many Western countries is a subtle structural mechanism that disadvantages people of ethnic minority origin in schools and higher education institutions, as well as in employment, workplaces, and access to life chances—while privileging people of dominant ethnic and racial communities.

God does not instigate afflictions and discrimination against His faithful children on account of their community background or social identity. As a matter of fact, God's major distinction with regard to humanity is between the redeemed in Christ and those who have not accepted His free plan of redemption through Christ. These two categories are alternatively called the saved and unsaved, or the children of the kingdom of light and those of the kingdom of darkness.

Speaking of the children of light in his letter to the church in Asia Minor, Apostle Peter reminded believers:

> **But you are a chosen people, a royal priesthood, a holy nation, God's special possession**, that you may declare the praises of him who called you out of darkness into his wonderful light. **Once you were not a people, but now you are the people of God**; once you had not received mercy, but now you have received mercy.
>
> *1 Peter 2:9-10, NIV*

It is important to recognize our new identity in Christ from God's perspective. Christians have a transformed special identity in Christ as the people of God.

While God makes a clear-cut distinction between His redeemed children and those who are not His, the Apostle Paul reminded the church in Galatia that, among the redeemed, God does not make any distinction on the basis of race, ethnicity, nationality or gender:

> **So, in Christ Jesus you are all children of God through faith,** for all of you who were baptized into Christ have clothed yourselves with Christ. **There is neither Jew nor Gentile, neither slave nor free, nor is there male and female, for you are all one in Christ Jesus. If you belong to Christ, then you are Abraham's seed, and heirs according to the promise.**
>
> *Galatians 3:26-29, NIV*

The enemy is spiritually behind the devious malpractices of negative discrimination, persecution and victimization of people, within or outside the body of Christ, and for whatever reason—whether because of one's racial, ethnic, gender or any other social identity. Christians should not encourage or promote such discrimination, lest we would be abetting the work of the devil.

The God of heaven and earth is a God of justice and has nothing but disapproval for discrimination or persecution of people based on their community background or social identity. Righteousness and justice are the foundations of God's throne, as the Bible declares, while mercy and truth are principles of His divine nature.

Understanding and Fighting the Battles of Life

Martin Luther King Jr and his fellow African-American folks fought several battles they had inherited from their forefathers, all because of their racial origin; and their descendants are still fighting those same battles in their neighbourhoods, workplaces and cities. The indigenous communities in Canada, USA, Mexico—in fact, the entire American continent—are also fighting many survivalist battles, again because of their community of origin and identity.

In many Western cities and residential neighbourhoods, there are communities where, as a teenager or young adult, you would have to fight twice as hard to avoid using hard drugs, joining a violent street gang, or ultimately going to jail for antisocial behaviours or criminal activities. There are believed to be more than 200 notorious criminal gangs, each bearing a distinctive nickname, that have collectively drawn into their ranks thousands of young people scattered across the deprived residential suburbs of present-day London.[20] In many poor African countries such as Ethiopia, Kenya and Nigeria, there are certain communities where impoverished young people have to fight twice as hard to escape being trafficked to the Middle East or Europe for prostitution and other kinds of degrading lifestyles.

As a social scientist, I am acquainted with diverse sociological explanations for these problems; but, as a minister of the gospel, I am also aware that the devil is behind these evils, as part of his universal agenda to steal, to kill, and to destroy. We know from the Bible that there are "wicked spiritual kingdoms reigning in the heavenlies which negatively influence events and the affairs of people on earth,"[21] such as the spiritual Prince of Persia in *Daniel 10:10-20*, the spiritual king of Tyre in *Ezekiel 28:11-19*, and the spiritual Pharaoh, king of Egypt, in *Ezekiel 29:1-5*. In all these cases, there is a spiritual kingdom which is established above the earthly kingdom, a phenomenon described by Kenneth E. Hagin as "the double kingdom".[22]

Problems and struggles associated with community background are not new. They have been there throughout history, even in the days of the Bible. The Hebrews were sojourners and later slaves for over 400 years in Egypt, where they faced brutal oppression and degradation at the hands of their Egyptian taskmasters. It took deliverance by the mighty hand of God and judgment over the rulers, people and gods of Egypt to put the captivity of the Hebrews to an end.

In the books of Judges and the major prophets in the Bible, we read about the Israelites being frequently handed over to their enemies, who oppressed, persecuted and sometimes enslaved them as a punishment for their collectively walking in sinful rebellion against God. Interestingly, oftentimes when they repented and God had delivered them, the Lord would then turn around to punish the same heathen nations He had allowed or used to chastise His people. The heathen nations were often punished for over-afflicting Israel when God was angry with them and for their own wickedness. The Bible is replete with God's wrath and judgment against different nations and communities for their abominable iniquities.

At the individual level, one of the ways to handle discrimination and persecution stemming from your community background is to affirm by faith that, regardless of your social identity, nobody can push you out of your divine inheritance and that you *will* enjoy the good of the land of your habitation because "the earth *is* the Lord's, and all its fullness, the world and those who dwell therein" (*Psalm 24:1*). Be determined in your heart to trust, obey and serve the Lord, and He will establish and prosper you in any land He takes you to. *Isaiah 1:19* gives us this assurance: "If you are willing and obedient, you will eat the good things of the land." In addition, you should also be determined to spiritually contend with the enemy to possess your possession and divine portion in the land, praying diverse kinds of prayers, supported by relevant scriptures.

Besides praying, you may also need to take appropriate action: lodging official complaints, following wise counsel, seeking legal redress, participating in campaigns for justice; such actions have often proved effective in pulling down strongholds of discrimination and oppression against different communities in modern history. Ensure that you are a loyal, law-abiding citizen and always give your best to your country and to your work, so that in due season the Lord can reward you with the best provisions and opportunities of the land:

> And whatever you do, do it heartily, as to the Lord and not to men, knowing that from the Lord you will receive the reward of the inheritance; for you serve the Lord Christ. But he who does wrong will be repaid for what he has done, and there is no partiality.
>
> *Colossians 3:23-25*

(3) Destiny

Satan fights everybody's destiny. However, the greater your destiny, the greater the battles you are likely to fight to have it established because Satan will resist you. God has a good destiny for everyone; but, in a natural sense, some people's destinies are greater than others. If your destiny is to be your country's Prime Minister, for instance, you have a greater but not necessarily more important destiny than if you were destined to be a cabinet minister or watch repairer. The destiny of the Prime Minister of the United Kingdom, for instance, will impact the entire country of 67 million people; but the destiny of a watch repairer may impact the wellbeing of just some thousands of people throughout his or her career. Let us consider a few examples of Bible characters with great destinies:

(i) **Moses** had a great destiny—to lead and deliver the children of Israel from Egypt after over 400 years of captivity. In a bid to stop this from happening, the devil laid an ambush to eliminate Moses before he was even born. The devil instigated Pharaoh to issue a decree to kill all the male children born of Hebrew women. The target was to prevent the emergence of a deliverer for the Hebrews. The devil knew that a deliverer was likely to emerge after 400 years of captivity, because God had revealed the duration of the captivity to Abraham (*Genesis 15:13-16*).

When God miraculously saved baby Moses, the enemy tried another tactic: biding his time until Moses had grown up, he then instigated him to kill an Egyptian unlawfully, thereby forcing him into exile in the land of the Midianites. There, for the next 40 years, Moses worked as a shepherd for his father-in-law—and if the devil had his way, he would have gone on doing so for the rest of his life. But God foiled the devil's schemes.

(ii) **Many mothers** who had the destiny of producing great covenant vessels of God were barren for many years. The enemy blocked their wombs because of their sons' great destinies: **Sarah** (Isaac's mother), **Rebekah** (Jacob's mother), **Rachel** (Joseph's mother), **the wife of Manoah** (Samson's mother), **Elizabeth** (mother of John the Baptist). The greater your destiny, the more battles you are likely to fight because the devil wants to abort that destiny.

(iii) **David** was destined to become Israel's greatest king. But, for about 15 years before that happened, he faced severe tribulations and battles, from the day God announced through the prophet Samuel that he was a man after His own heart (*1 Samuel 13:14*). First, the devil sent a lion and a bear after David and his flock, but he tore the two beasts apart with his bare hands; he later fought the Philistine war veteran Goliath and won. His greatest and longest battle was when Saul the king of Israel pursued him with his large armies for probably more than eight years, seeking to kill him and abort his destiny of becoming Israel's king.

It is instructive that David had seven older brothers who did not face any recorded serious personal battles, apparently because none of them had a comparably great destiny. If your battles seem to be bigger than your siblings' and you all have the same spiritual and social foundation, it could be because, like David and Joseph in the Bible, your destiny is potentially the greatest in your family.

(iv) **Samson** evidently had a great destiny to deliver the children of Israel from the hands of the Philistines, who had oppressed them for 40 years (see *Judges 13-16*). But Satan confused Samson's heart to love only Philistine women and ultimately used one of them (Delilah) to waste his destiny. Here was a man with such a great destiny that he even had an angel descending from heaven to prophesy his birth; but he died as a prisoner in the hands of his enemies, with his two eyes gouged out.

(v) **Jeremiah** had such a great destiny that, as soon as God announced his calling as His prophet (see Jeremiah 1), the battles against him started. The kings and prophets and priests in Israel fought him bitterly, conspired against him, threw him into prison, and tried to starve him to death. When that failed, they cast him into a deep, miry pit, hoping he would die a miserable death.

Jeremiah was once so depressed and exasperated by the massive attacks on him that he cursed the day he was born and even questioned why he did not die in his mother's womb (see *Jeremiah 20:14-18*). Satan's game plan is to fight your destiny and frustrate you to the point where you could denounce God, if possible, or kill yourself and end up in hell.

(vi) ***The Lord Jesus Christ*** had a great destiny as Saviour of the whole world. Jesus faced enormous battles from birth, with the devil laying an ambush to kill Him soon after his birth was announced to Herod, the Roman-appointed king of Judea (see *Matthew 2*). But God delivered the baby Jesus by warning his earthly foster father Joseph of the impending danger, and the family fled to Egypt. From the time Jesus started his ministry at the age of 30, the Pharisees and religious leaders plotted on several occasions to kill Him; but all their schemes failed because it was not yet His time to die, and the devil had no claim on Him as He was sinless. It was only when one of His disciples connived with the Pharisees to betray and arrest Him that Jesus voluntarily handed Himself over to die for the redemption of the world. The greater your destiny, the bigger your battles. But if you trust in the Lord who is the author of your destiny, you will surely prevail: "this is the victory that overcomes the world, even our faith" (*1 John 5:4*).

What, therefore, is the solution to the battles of destiny? It is this: ***looking up to Jesus the Author and Finisher of our faith, and constantly leaning on Him for help***.

> Therefore we also, **since we are surrounded by so great a cloud of witnesses, let us lay aside every weight, and the sin which so easily ensnares** *us,* **and let us run with endurance the race that is set before us, looking unto Jesus, the author and finisher of** *our* **faith, who for the joy that was set before Him endured the cross, despising the shame, and has sat down at the right hand of the throne of God.**
>
> *Hebrews 12:1-2*
>
> **So do not throw away your confidence; it will be richly rewarded. You need to persevere so that when you have done the will of God, you will receive what he has promised.** For, "In just a little while, he who is coming will come and will not delay." And "But my righteous one will live by faith. And I take no pleasure in the one who shrinks back." **But we do not belong to those who shrink back and are destroyed,** but to those who have faith and are saved.
>
> *Hebrews 10:35-39*

(4) The choices we make in life

Every day we make choices in life and the choices we make impact heavily on our destinies, whether positively or negatively. **The choices we make also determine the battles we fight in life and the possible outcomes of those battles.**

Our choices can have far-reaching consequences. Adam and Eve, the first created human beings, made the first catastrophic choice on earth when they fell into temptation instigated by the devil. Mankind has not yet recovered fully, even today, from the consequences of their decision to disobey God, because *choices have consequences*. And then there was Abraham, who yielded to the prodding of his wife Sarah to have a child with Hagar (Sarah's Egyptian maid), and the consequences of that choice have trans-generationally affected the descendants of Hagar and Sarah ever since.

Where we choose to live can also lead to grave consequences. In Genesis 19 we have the story of Lot, who chose to settle in Sodom because of his greed and covetousness, and that decision ultimately spelt doom for his destiny. And Ruth 1 tells us about Elimelech, who chose to migrate from the land of Judah to Moab in search of greener pastures, taking along with him his wife and two sons; but that decision cut short his life—as well as the lives of his two sons—and left his wife Naomi a wretched widow. So, the choice we make about where to live is important and does have implications for the battles we may face in life.

Who we choose as our partner in a sexual or conjugal union matters too. Samson rejected all the beautiful women in Israel and repeatedly chose to love Philistine women who were unbelievers under the terms of the Old Covenant; and that decision cost him his destiny. Even David, the man after God's heart, made the catastrophic choice of going after another man's wife; and that wrong decision provoked God's judgment against him, costing him the lives of three or four of his children and causing him to lose his kingdom for a few years, with his son seeking to kill him. Choices have consequences.

Joseph, on the other hand, made a godly choice not to sleep with his master Potiphar's wife. That wise decision initially caused him to be framed, falsely accused, and sentenced to jail for about ten years.

He suffered for a sin he did not commit, but God did not forsake him and, after about ten years of suffering, God delivered him from prison and made him ruler over Egypt. It is better to suffer persecution for a godly choice you have made than to make a sinful choice which you will certainly suffer for sooner or later. When you suffer for doing good, wisely trusting God, He will vindicate you; but when you suffer for doing evil, you may not suffer with divine commendation.

Jehoshaphat, king of Judah, was a righteous man but he made repeated choices of aligning with the wicked, which provoked God's judgment against him. You cannot be a righteous man or woman and make the wicked—all those who hate and despise God—your best friends and allies, which was what Jehoshaphat did, time and again, until he wore out God's mercy:

(i) *Jehoshaphat made a marriage alliance with the wicked King Ahab of Israel:*

> Jehoshaphat had riches and honour in abundance; and by marriage he allied himself with Ahab. After some years he went down to *visit* Ahab in Samaria; and Ahab killed sheep and oxen in abundance for him and the people who were with him, and persuaded him to go up *with him* to Ramoth Gilead. So Ahab king of Israel said to Jehoshaphat king of Judah, "Will you go with me *against* Ramoth Gilead?" And he answered him, "I *am* as you *are,* and my people as your people; *we will be* with you in the war."
>
> *2 Chronicles 18:1-3*

(ii) *God rebuked Jehoshaphat for allying with Ahab but showed him mercy:*

> Then Jehoshaphat the king of Judah returned safely to his house in Jerusalem. And Jehu the son of Hanani the seer went out to meet him, and said to King Jehoshaphat, "Should you help the wicked and love those who hate the Lord? Therefore, the wrath of the Lord *is* upon you. Nevertheless, good things are found in you, in that you have removed the wooden images from the land, and have prepared your heart to seek God."
>
> *2 Chronicles 19:1-3*

(iii) ***Jehoshaphat made a business alliance with the wicked son of Ahab, King Ahaziah of Israel, and the alliance provoked God's judgment:***

> After this Jehoshaphat king of Judah allied himself with Ahaziah king of Israel, who acted very wickedly. And he allied himself with him to make ships to go to Tarshish, and they made the ships in Ezion Geber. But Eliezer the son of Dodavah of Mareshah prophesied against Jehoshaphat, saying, "Because you have allied yourself with Ahaziah, the Lord has destroyed your works." Then the ships were wrecked, so that they were not able to go to Tarshish.
>
> 2 Chronicles 20:35-37

Choices have consequences.

If we look at human existence from the viewpoint of the Bible, it is vital to understand that God has set choices before us, but He urges us to choose wisely, that we and our children may live. *We need to take heed of the following declaration that the Lord made to Israel:*

> I call heaven and earth as witnesses today against you, *that* **I have set before you life and death, blessing and cursing; therefore choose life, that both you and your descendants may live;** that you may love the Lord your God, that you may obey His voice, and that you may cling to Him, for He *is* your life and the length of your days; and that you may dwell in the land which the Lord swore to your fathers, to Abraham, Isaac, and Jacob, to give them.
>
> Deuteronomy 30:19-20

The greatest choice you can make on earth is to know the Lord, seek Him and passionately serve Him, together with your household. It was this great choice that Joshua challenged the Israelites to make in his time, unequivocally declaring his own choice to serve the Lord, together with his household:

> "Now therefore, fear the Lord, serve Him in sincerity and in truth, and put away the gods which your fathers served on the other side of the river and in Egypt. Serve the Lord!

> And if it seems evil to you to serve the Lord, choose for yourselves this day whom you will serve, whether the gods which your fathers served that *were* on the other side of the river, or the gods of the Amorites, in whose land you dwell. But as for me and my house, we will serve the Lord."
>
> *Joshua 24:14-15*

Serving the Lord is profitable in this life and in eternity. Many Christians do not want to obey and serve the Lord; they only want His blessings. But the Lord is a true rewarder of those that diligently seek and serve Him:

> You shall serve [only] the Lord your God, and He shall bless your bread and water. I will also remove sickness from among you. No one shall suffer miscarriage or be barren in your land; I will fulfil the number of your days. I will send My terror ahead of you, and I will throw into confusion all the people among whom you come, and I will make all your enemies turn their backs to you [in flight]. I will send hornets ahead of you which shall drive out the Hivite, the Canaanite, and the Hittite before you.
>
> *Exodus 23:25-28, AMP*

The Lord demands that we obey and serve Him; and those who truly do, despite any temporary challenges and setbacks, shall ultimately "spend their days in prosperity and their years in pleasures" (*Job 36:11*).

(5) The inherent conflict between the flesh and the spirit

There is an inherent war that constantly rages in every believer's life: the war between the flesh and the spirit. How you regularly resolve this invisible personal war has consequences for many other battles you may face in life. Apostle Paul captured this inherent personal battle in every believer's life with this exhortation: "But I say, walk by the Spirit, and do not gratify the desires of the flesh. **For the desires of the flesh are against the Spirit, and the desires of the Spirit are against the flesh; for these are opposed to each other,** to prevent you from doing what you would" (*Galatians 5:16-17, RSV*).

The flesh represents the ungodly desires, inclinations and tendencies of the fallen nature of man, which are invariably contrary to the ways of God. The Bible declares that nothing good dwells in our flesh and that it is (spiritual) death for a Christian to set his mind on the flesh or live according to the dictates of the flesh. The mind that is set on the flesh is hostile to God, does not submit to God's commandments, and cannot please God.

The flesh is in constant conflict with the indwelling Holy Spirit in the life of every believer; and the war against the flesh is a tougher battle to wage than the battle against the devil, which Jesus has already won for us. As a matter of fact, most times the devil gets at believers through the weaknesses of their flesh.

The solution to winning this inherent battle against the flesh lies in our developing the capacity to live and walk by the leading of the indwelling Holy Spirit, so that we do not gratify the desires of the flesh. As the preceding Bible passage indicates, Christians are not to do whatever they want but to live according to the Word of God and to yield to the leading of the Holy Spirit. To do whatever you want, against the desires and leading of the Holy Spirit, amounts to walking in the flesh and grieving the Holy Spirit. To walk constantly by the Spirit requires crucifying your flesh daily (dying to self) and surrendering your personal will to God in all circumstances.

It is certainly not the easiest work to walk by the Spirit, but that is the walk for which every believer has been saved and called to walk. This is a good prayer pointer for every child of God—asking the Lord to help you to walk by the Spirit and not to gratify the desires of the flesh. We are practically at war with the flesh and the devil in this life, but it is a war that the grace of redemption and the gift of the Holy Spirit have equipped us to win, if we are determined in our hearts to prevail. Whenever you slip and fall in this walk and fight of faith, do not remain down. Pick up yourself and ask the Lord for mercy and the grace to continue until victory is eternally secured.

> **Box 5.1: Pause to actively pray these prayer pointers**
>
> 1) My heavenly Father, open my spiritual eyes to perceive every mysterious battle I may have inherited from my mother's womb or family background, which I know not, IJN.
> 2) I command the inherited spiritual battles hindering my life and destiny to be ended by the power in the Blood of redemption, IJN.
> 3) By the power in the Blood of Jesus, I break every resistance of the adversary against the manifestation of my destiny, IJN.
> 4) By the power in the Blood of redemption, I command every aspect of my destiny to be loosed from the stranglehold of the forces of darkness, IJN.
> 5) Lord, may you forgive me for all the times I have grieved the indwelling Holy Spirit, IJN.
> 6) By the mercies in the Blood of redemption, Lord, may you set me free from the penalties of all my sins, IJN.
> 7) I command every affliction of the forces of darkness due to my past sins to be ended now, IJN.
> 8) Lord, help me to always overcome the temptation to walk in disobedience to God's will, IJN.
> 9) My heavenly Father, may you show me mercy and set me free from the consequences of the bad choices and decisions I have made in life, IJN.
> 10) My heavenly Father, help me to learn how to live and walk by the direction and guidance of the indwelling Holy Spirit, IJN.
> 11) Lord, I thank you for all your answers to my prayers, IJN.

A New Destiny of Unlimited Possibilities

Finally, let me make the most important point about fighting the battles of life. It is important to understand that, regardless of one's sociocultural heritage or personal circumstances, salvation—the new birth in Christ—confers a new destiny of unlimited possibilities upon the redeemed. I have illustrated this point in greater detail in a different book I published in 2015 titled *Understanding Divine Destiny*.

This new destiny of the redeemed in Christ gives every believer a commanding advantage in all the battles of life, no matter how deep-rooted or complex these battles might seem. There is no natural disadvantage any child of God may have that cannot be supernaturally corrected and positively transformed by the same Spirit, power and grace that have brought salvation to us; this is the power of Christ in us. Too often, the so-called natural disadvantages could temporarily make the journey tougher at the beginning; but, as we grow in spiritual knowledge and work out our salvation in the fear of God, the grace of unlimited destiny will launch us to greater heights, possibilities and accomplishments in all aspects of our lives.

Confirming the destiny of unlimited possibilities of the redeemed, Jesus declared that whoever believes in Him will do the works that He did, and even greater works, by the power of the Holy Spirit that He gives from the Father. Jesus did immeasurable great works of healing, deliverance of the demonically oppressed, raising the dead, teaching, and other diverse miracles. Anyone who believes in the Lord can do greater works, implying that there are no limits to what the redeemed could potentially achieve by the power of God, regardless of their sociocultural antecedents. Similarly, Jesus told a man who brought his demon-possessed son to Him for healing that "If you can believe, **all things *are* possible** to him who believes" (*Mark 9:23*). Again, this points to the unlimited supernatural destiny of the believer.

As we walk with the Lord, all things are possible, according to His divine will, and no good thing does the Lord withhold from those who walk uprightly. There are also no limits to the type of healing, favours, blessings, and deliverance miracles that the redeemed could personally seek and receive in his or her lifetime. It takes knowledge, faith, obedience and persistence to walk and grow in the destiny of unlimited possibilities in Christ.

Chapter 6

Living by Your Own Faith — Personal Faith

The Bible tells us that faith is confidence in what we hope for and the assurance that God, who is Spirit, is working in the spirit realm, even though we cannot see it.[23] "A better word for faith," teaches God's illustrious servant and faith preacher, Lester Sumrall, is "trust"—"how much faith do you have *in God and His word*?" — meaning, "how much *trust* do you have *in God and His word*?"[24]

Having a believing knowledge of what God's Word says is the foundation of true faith in *El Shaddai* or the All Sufficient God. To live a victorious life, our faith must be based on believing what God's Word says, not on our natural senses (how we feel; what we see, smell, hear, touch or taste), the opinions of men or a doctor's clinical report. Every believer has a personal responsibility to disbelieve and combat any views or thoughts that run counter to what God's Word says. God's Word contains His commandments, ordinances, covenants, principles, promises and plans for anyone interested in a relationship with Him, as well as His eternal prophecies, sacred songs of worship, and the history of His dealings with humanity. In short, God's Word is His divine will.

True faith in God must be based on God's Word alone, because His Word is eternal truth, righteous and dependable. No other written or spoken words can be as trustworthy as God's Word. Believing what God says about any condition, as biblical heroes of faith like Abraham and Noah did, is a necessary step or process that must precede the physical manifestation of one's expected desire or prayer request. When Christians don't have the true knowledge of God's Word deeply rooted and believed in their hearts, operating in faith becomes difficult. And when it becomes difficult to operate in faith in God because our relationship with Him is not grounded in His revealed Word, we make ourselves more vulnerable to doubt, unbelief, failure, frustration, irritability, instability, false doctrines, a weak prayer life, and being easily overcome by diverse temptations of the devil. "We cannot always feel God's presence or understand His guidance," writes Mary Fairchild (2021), "it takes faith to find God and faith *in His word* to keep our eyes on Him so that we persevere until the end."[25]

The good news is that we are saved by faith in God, and every saved Christian can live and walk by faith, regardless of one's present circumstances or level of faith. The Christian faith walk is akin to a crawling baby learning to stand on his feet and walk. He could fall many times, make wobbling steps; nevertheless, as long as He does not give up but keeps trying, he will get better at it and grow stronger, especially if he leans on the tutelage of a grown-up guardian. The indwelling Holy Spirit is given to every believer as a Helper in our faith walk and, therefore, we have to lean on Him. The body of Christ is equipped with pastors, teachers, evangelists and many more serving in other ministerial offices—and we have to learn from them.

Renowned American televangelist Andrew Wommack makes an instructive comparison of the Christian faith walk to the history of mankind's experiments with inventing and flying an airplane. Reverend Wommack (n.d.) remarked that, during the experimental years of trying to build an aircraft, many people scoffed at the idea of flying—in a similar way in which so many ridicule the faith message today. However, after repeated failed attempts spanning many years, a powered airplane was successfully invented, and today the flying aircraft has been perfected because of the perseverance of those who believed against all odds in the possibility that the laws of aerodynamics could help them devise a flying vessel. Wommack concluded that the law of faith, which created everything, is a thousand times surer than the laws of aerodynamics; but, regrettably, the knowledge of God and how faith works, which is hidden in the Word of God, has not been discovered by many.[26]

In our walk with God, each of us needs to have our own faith, or what is alternatively called "personal faith". You are saved by your own faith; you work out your salvation by your own faith; you are justified by your own faith; you live by your own faith; you die by your own faith; and you make it to heaven or hell as an outcome of your own faith. This makes it important that you develop and grow your own faith. Somebody else's faith can sometimes help you, but to a very limited extent. Somebody else's faith and prayers can help you obtain some miracles, some of the time, but not all miracles, and not all the time. Somebody else's faith and prayers can help you get healed, but it may not help you to sustain that healing if the devil brings back the affliction. Somebody else's faith and prayers can help you get a job, but it may not help you keep the job or get promoted on the job. Somebody else's faith and prophetic declaration can help you get married, but it may not help you sustain the marriage. Hence, you certainly need to work on growing your own faith, as well as living and prevailing in prayer and in life by your personal faith.

Acquiring an understanding and a mentality of prevailing faith helps you, along with prevailing prayers, to consistently obtain your desired or expected outcomes, in accordance with divine will and purpose. Faith in general does not exempt you from experiencing the problems and challenges of daily life; it essentially helps you to prevail and overcome them. *Hebrews 11:6* tells us that "without faith *it is* impossible to please *Him,* for he who comes to God must believe that He is, and *that* He is a rewarder of those who diligently seek Him." Without faith, you can't please God; and when you can't please God and seek Him diligently, there are many rewards you can't get from God and many of your prayers that He will not answer.

Without getting, developing and growing your own faith, you may not stay in any church for long, especially if the adversary bombards you with difficult problems that your faith cannot handle. You will constantly be under the impression that you are saddled with those persistent problems because your pastor or church does not possess enough spiritual power to solve them; so, you may end up moving from one church to another, continuously searching for solutions. What the devil will not remind you, in such a situation, is that some other people with similar challenges, or even much harder ones, may have seen God solve their problems in the same church. There are, of course, times when a church one attends might be part of the problem; but there are other times when one's lack of faith, commitment or obedience to God could be the primary problem.

Jesus repeatedly rebuked His disciples for their faithlessness or little faith. In other words, despite being physically present with Jesus, who could solve every problem, each of them still needed to develop and operate his own faith and not continue to depend on Jesus' faith as Lord. In any case, Jesus wasn't always going to be physically present with them.

> For the vision is yet for the appointed [future] time. It hurries toward the goal [of fulfilment]; it will not fail. Even though it delays, wait [patiently] for it, because it will certainly come; it will not delay. Look at the proud one, His soul is not right within him, **But the righteous will live by his faith** [in the true God].
>
> *Habakkuk 2:3-4, AMP*

Speaking through the prophet Habakkuk, God demanded that, in order to await the appointed time for the fulfilment of His heavenly vision, the righteous shall live by his own faith, not the faith of the prophet or some other person. This Bible passage, among many others, highlights the need for personal faith. Faith is fundamentally an individual or personal thing, even though two or more persons or even an entire congregation or fellowship could jointly exercise their faith to achieve the desired results.

I wish to define faith or personal faith as "the act of believing God and His Word unconditionally, and the corresponding confession you make and actions you take in the expectation that God is committed to performing His word." Personal faith also extends to the domain of submitting or yielding obediently to God, that His will be done. God is Spirit, and it is by our personal faith that we individually know Him and relate to Him: "and those who worship Him must worship in spirit and truth" (*John 4:24*).

Key Points to Explain Personal Faith

Renowned Bible teacher Kenneth E. Hagin gives us an incisive explanation of personal faith, describing it as a living "spiritual force" with extraordinarily powerful *logos* and *rhema* dimensions. Citing *Romans 10:17*, Hagin affirms that biblical faith is a spiritual force which comes by our repeatedly hearing the Word of God.

Hearing the *logos* or written Word of God develops faith inside of us. And, as we believe and speak the *logos* Word of God, it somehow becomes a *rhema* Word of God to us—*rhema* meaning "the spoken word."[27] Let me proceed further to outline some key points to explain personal faith:

(1) What you consistently believe in your heart and confess with your mouth centrally defines your faith

This spiritual principle of belief and confession is the key to receiving from God the free salvation that Christ has fully paid for all: "if you confess with your mouth the Lord Jesus and believe in your heart that God has raised Him from the dead, you will be saved. For with the heart, one believes unto righteousness, and with the mouth confession is made unto salvation" (*Romans 10:9-10*). This principle, which is applicable to receiving the grace of salvation through faith, also applies to other things we receive from God or accomplish in partnership with Him—the "better things… that accompany salvation" (*Hebrews 6:9*). In explaining to His disciples the operational mechanics of faith, Jesus said to them:

> **Have faith in God.** For assuredly, I say to you, **whoever says to this mountain,** "Be removed and be cast into the sea," and does not doubt in his heart, **but believes that those things he says will be done, he will have whatever he says.**
>
> *Mark 11:22-23*

As Jesus explained, faith in God works through a combination of what we believe in our heart and say undoubtingly with our mouth. Ultimately, what you receive is whatever you say, not exclusively what you believe —making the saying part as important as the believing part in the birthing of miracles. Many believers tend to lay more emphasis on the believing part of faith, while disregarding the saying or confessing part, or even saying things that contradict what they claim to believe. This is inappropriate. Both the believing and saying parts are of vital importance. The believing part is probably easier than the confessional part, which requires verbalized consistency and boldness.

Sometime in 2002, I challenged a colleague of mine to a spiritual healing contest. She had suffered from severe migraine for many years, frequently complaining about her distressing pains. She lived on constant painkillers. As she whined again and again in the midst of our breaktime conversation about her throbbing headache and pain, I told her that, if she would receive Jesus Christ into her life as Lord and Saviour, and I prayed for her, Jesus would heal her immediately of the migraine. There were four other female colleagues around when I issued the challenge. The lady quickly reversed the order of the offer I proposed, saying that, if I prayed for her first and Jesus healed her, she would immediately give her life to Christ. The rest of the women, all of whom I had preached to repeatedly, took sides with her, saying that, if I prayed and Jesus healed her instantly, they would all believe my gospel to be true.

I accepted their challenge without thinking. It was the first time I was accepting an open contest to prove that Jesus performed miracles as Lord and Saviour—but by no means the last time. As the lady spontaneously stood up for prayer while all the other women stared at me, convulsed with curiosity, I quickly laid my hand on her head and started praying. There was a sudden surge of doubt in my mind as I prayed. "Suppose this miracle does not happen when I finish praying, what would I say to these women about Jesus, in whose name and healing power I have boasted?" I struggled to suppress my inner doubts while making bold declarations of faith with my mouth. I loudly rebuked the spirit behind the migraine and commanded that the lady be healed, praying further for the Lord to use the miracle to prove Himself to her and all the others in the room, in Jesus' name.

Before I could ask her how she felt, not being sure in my mind what to expect, she gleefully screamed, "It is gone, I am healed, I am healed." She reported that she experienced something jumping out of her head when I had completed the prayer, and all the migraine symptoms vanished from her head and body. I felt ecstatic, unburdened, vindicated, but truly as astonished as any one of them because of the struggling doubt in my mind while I was praying. Nowadays, by the grace of God, I no longer entertain such doubts when I pray for people to receive healing or other miracles.

"You have to give your life to Jesus, now that He has healed you," I gladly and more confidently declared to the lady. Her curious friends and colleagues, who had watched the five-minute miracle drama, were all speechless but the lady declined to give her life to Jesus Christ, saying that she needed to watch it for a couple of days to be sure that the healing was real. That "couple of days" turned into weeks, the healing was still real, but she refused to give her life to Christ. After about thirty days of refusing to fulfil her own part of the bargain, she lost the miracle.

In Christ Jesus, God has made all grace abound towards His redeemed children, that they may always have all things in abundance for every good work; however, all that God has made available is only accessible by faith. All the promises of God in the scriptures are receivable by faith, and the starting point of faith is what you believe in your heart and confess with your mouth. What you do not believe, you can hardly receive—or retain, even if you happen to receive it. If, for instance, you do not believe that, as a Christian, you can live sickness-free all the days of your life, you will hardly walk in that grace or receive it. Conversely, you can believe and confess it without receiving it; but the potential to receive it is there for everyone who believes and consistently says it.

The same thing applies to all other provisions of scripture, such as receiving the gifts of the Holy Spirit, finding a spouse, breaking the yoke of barrenness or sterility in marriage, passing exams, finding a job, and starting or prospering in your own business. For your confession to be positively consistent with faith in God and in His power, it must not only align with what you believe but also with what you think, say, and meditate on: "For as he thinks in his heart, so *is* he" (*Proverbs 23:7*). Whatever preoccupies your thoughts and imagination will invariably find expression in what you confess.

(2) Your personal faith must include a vital work dimension that helps to materialize or deliver the expected outcome you believe in your heart and confess with your mouth

As captured in *James 2:17-18*: "Thus also faith by itself, if it does not have works, is dead... Show me your faith without your works, and I will show you my faith by my works."

James makes it clear that there is "living faith" and there is "dead faith", which correspond respectively to "faith with works" and "faith without works". It is the vital works or actions you take, in line with the Word of God you have heard, received or believed, that give life to faith, causing God to deliver the answer to your prayer or to perform the expected miracle. This is a simple principle that runs across most miracles in the Bible. When the prophet Elisha told the Syrian army general Naaman, who was leprous, to dip himself seven times in the River Jordan for his leprosy to be cured, it was not a therapeutic prescription that made any natural sense; but, to a person of faith, it makes supernatural sense. Naaman, despite his initial hesitation and preconceived ideas about how the man of God should have acted to heal him, was persuaded to take the required action according to the words spoken by the prophet of God. And, as he acted by faith in accordance with the instructions of the prophet, Naaman was completely healed by God.

When the Apostle Paul was preaching in Lystra, he perceived that a man crippled from birth, who was in the audience listening to him, had the faith to be healed; and so, Paul said to him "with a loud voice, 'Stand up on your feet.' And he jumped up and *began* to walk" (*Acts 14:10, AMP*). Paul issued a command to the crippled man to act on his own faith. The man acted on Paul's command by spontaneously jumping or leaping up, apparently without thinking about the lifeless or weak state of his legs. It was while the crippled man was *in the process of initiating a seemingly impossible action* by his own faith that the Lord instantly healed him and he began to walk. Had he not responded to Paul's faith and command by taking the required positive action, the Lord would not have healed him. He received his miracle because of his vital *work dimension* of faith; what T. L. Osborn calls "dynamic faith."[28]

Every blessing of God that we could possibly need or earnestly desire is available to us in the Bible, but there are scriptural principles we must act on to receive them. An adept study of the scriptures will help you understand the conditions that appertain to the diverse promises and provisions of grace in the Bible. There is no grace or blessing you seek today as a child of God that people have not sought or received in the days of the Bible or previous generations.

What they did to walk in those graces you desire today is all revealed in the Bible to anyone who wants to learn to do the same. It is also important to mention that (apart from specific keys to receiving God's promises) seeking and serving God passionately and wholeheartedly—being determined to make costly sacrifices for the sake of advancing His kingdom on earth—is a master key that can unlock any blessing. It is only a matter of time!

> Therefore do not worry, saying, "What shall we eat?" or "What shall we drink?" or "What shall we wear?" For after all these things the Gentiles seek. For your heavenly Father knows that you need all these things. **But seek first the kingdom of God and His righteousness, and all these things shall be added to you**.
>
> *Matthew 6:31-33*

Christians are called to seek God, not things. The things we desire are added to us as benefits and rewards for diligently seeking and serving God. This is the key work dimension of faith in God and His Word.

> **For God is not unjust. He will not forget how hard you have worked for him** and **how you have shown your love to him by caring for other believers, as you still do.**
>
> *Hebrews 6:10, NLT*

Human beings can forget and disregard your costly sacrifices, commitment and love towards them, but not the righteous and loving God of the universe.

(3) Your personal faith depends on how much of the Word of God you know, understand, believe, confess and apply

God is Spirit, and so is His Word; our faith in God must rest on His written word in the Bible (*logos*) and His spoken or revealed word to you personally (*rhema*). The latter must be validated by the former. The Word of God is God's spiritual food, meant to be eaten by His children for spiritual nourishment and sustenance. It is also the spiritual seed we need to birth our desired physical results. There are relevant words of God for every circumstance or problem we may face in life at individual, family, group and other (higher) levels.

It is therefore of utmost importance that you study the Word and also gain knowledge of how to appropriate and deploy it in prayer to achieve your desired results. The Word of God is the most powerful force on earth. God created the entire universe by His spoken Word, upholding all things by the power of His Word.

God has made more than 800 promises in the Bible to mankind. Most of these promises come with certain conditions attached—among them, several blessings for obeying His commandments and curses for acting in disobedience. Bible commentators like Robert Oliver (2019) have described the blessings for obeying God's commandments as "positive promises" and the curses for disobeying Him as "negative promises". Many Christians feel a bit overwhelmed or confused about the biblical requirement to obey God's commandments because there are too many of them. The five books of Moses alone—Genesis to Deuteronomy—contain a total of 613 commandments, not just the famous ten commandments.[29] However, under the new covenant, Jesus reduced all of God's commandments to one, the commandment to love:

> A new commandment I give to you, that you love one another; as I have loved you, that you also love one another.
> *John 13:34*

Love is the new commandment of God. When we walk in love, we will not think evil against our neighbour or do harm to others or to society at large. Jesus elaborated further on this commandment to love, saying:

> "You shall love the Lord your God with all your heart, with all your soul, and with all your mind." This is *the* first and great commandment. And *the* second *is* like it: "You shall love your neighbour as yourself." On these two commandments hang all the Law and the Prophets.
> *Matthew 22:37-40*

To walk effectively in love, we have to be guided by the teachings of Jesus in the gospels and the letters or epistles of the apostles to the early churches in the New Testament.

Living by Your Own Faith—Personal Faith

God is committed to answering the prayers and declarations of faith that are based on His promises in the Bible. Let us imagine that you have the wealthiest man in the world as your best friend, and this fellow is highly compassionate, trustworthy and generous. He has made you a promise to help you any time you have a genuine need. If you were to wreck your car in an accident and genuinely needed a new one, and you asked your wealthy friend for help in accordance with his promise, he would be unlikely to refuse your request for a new car—even if the accident had clearly been caused by your own driving error. Your decision to ask this compassionate, wealthy friend for a car is within the remit of his promise and the applicable condition he gave you: namely, when you have a genuine need.

Now, consider this: if a good man is unlikely to fail you in this imagined circumstance—even though all humans are fallible and could unexpectedly disappoint you—then, all the more, the good God of the universe, whose power and resources are unlimited, will not fail you when you approach Him prayerfully, with faith anchored on His Bible promises. On the other hand, to step out of His promises and the necessary conditions or principles could make it more difficult for your faith to achieve the desired results.

(4) There are varied levels of personal faith

We are all at different levels of faith, but there are abundant opportunities and grace in Christ for every believer to grow in faith.

(i) *Some have **unbelief** or an **unbelieving heart***: starting with unbelief is ironic, because it is not really a level of faith but the opposite of it, and therefore doesn't do anybody any good. Many of the people we call unbelievers have unbelief in their hearts, but not all. Some believers who refuse to renew their minds according to God's Word could depart from the living God because of "an evil heart of unbelief" (*Hebrews 3:12*), especially those whose hearts have been "hardened through the deceitfulness of sin" (*Hebrews 3:13*). When Jesus was teaching in the synagogue at Nazareth, His hometown, He rebuked the congregants because of their unbelief and, on that occasion, "He did not do many mighty works there" (see *Matthew 13:53-58*).

In fact, the people were so infuriated by Jesus' rebuke that they led him out of the synagogue and would have destroyed him but for the mystique of his anointing. Unbelief could make folks, including religious folks in the synagogue or church, do many crazy or even devilish things against the truth. Apostle Paul urged the church in Thessalonica to pray for him and his missional team, that they "may be delivered from unreasonable and wicked men; for not all have faith" (*2 Thessalonians 3:2-4*). Many perverse and ungodly people have sold their souls to Satan to do evil and, as such, do not have the Bible-authorized faith in the true God.

(ii) *Jesus once rebuked his disciples for their **little faith***, when they were afraid of a storm at sea and thought they were perishing while He slept in the boat (*Mark 16:14*). On another occasion, Jesus contrasted the "little faith" of His disciples with a faith "as small as a mustard seed", which He said could move a mountain when effectively deployed (see *Matthew 17:20, NLT*).

(iii) Jesus said, concerning the Centurion who told Him not to bother going with Him to his house, but to just speak the word and his servant would be healed, *"I have not found such **great faith**, not even in Israel!"* (*Matthew 8:10*). The Centurion had great faith: "Then Jesus said to the centurion, 'Go your way; and as you have believed, *so* let it be done for you.' And his servant was healed that same hour" (*Matthew 8:13*).

(iv) Abraham waited many years for the covenant child promised by God; the Bible says he was not "weak in faith", despite his being almost a hundred years old and his wife Sarah nearly 90 years, with her womb dead. Instead, Abraham became "strong in faith, giving glory to God" (see *Romans 4:19-21*, KJV). It is this tested but defiant ***"strong faith"*** that birthed the miracle. Hence, personal faith can be weak or strong—***weak faith*** or ***strong faith***.

We are all at different levels of personal faith—no faith or unbelief; little faith; great faith; strong faith—but every believer must aspire to grow in their personal faith, and there are always abundant opportunities for growth. These various levels or varying measures of faith will be explained in greater detail in Chapter 7.

(5) Personal faith can become stagnant, may decline, and could even die

Personal faith dies when someone who has tasted the grace of salvation and seen the light of the gospel of Christ decides to abandon the Lord and go back to the world. According to *Hebrews 10:28-29*, such a person deserves severe punishment because he has trampled the Son of God underfoot, desecrated the blood of the covenant, and insulted the Spirit of grace. God does and could still restore backsliders while they remain alive on earth but, once they are dead, restoration becomes rather too late.

(6) In addition to having different levels of personal faith, believers also have different capacities for exercising faith in diverse circumstances

Some have developed their faith in God to a high level when it comes, for instance, to making money, but they cannot believe Him when it comes to divine healing, living above sicknesses and diseases, succeeding in marriage, raising godly children, travelling accident-free at all times, living above the magical attacks of witches and the wicked, and so forth. Some Christians believe in salvation, but their personal faith cannot accommodate many other provisions of the Bible, such as baptism of the Holy Spirit, rapture of the saints, raising the dead back to life, and resurrection of the just and unjust.

Mark 16:14 recounts how Jesus rebuked His disciples for their unbelief and hardness of heart concerning His resurrection, because they did not believe the account of those who had seen Him after He rose from the dead. So, it is important that we strive to grow our faith all-round and not only in just one aspect of life; otherwise, the devil will freely take advantage of us in all the areas where our personal faith is weak or hardened by unbelief.

(7) As Mediator of the new covenant, Jesus is the anchor of our personal faith journey

Faith is a spiritual force and, according to *Hebrews 12:2*, Jesus is the Author and Finisher of our faith. He authors our faith at the point of spiritual birth or salvation and He finishes it, if we endure till the end, when we transit to be with Him eternally; or, for the generation that will be privileged to experience the rapture, when He shall suddenly appear in the clouds of heaven to rapture the saints who are eagerly waiting for Him.

In between the Lord's authoring of your faith and finishing it, you have an individual responsibility to live by your own faith—to work out your salvation by faith and to pray without ceasing by faith. Ideally, this may necessitate following some set times for daily prayer, as was the practice among the early disciples, a beneficial tradition they inherited from Judaism. It is also every believer's responsibility to diligently seek and serve the Lord by faith, to hear and believe the Word of God by faith, to spread the soul-winning gospel by faith, to pray for the sick to receive their healing by faith, and to cast out demons by faith.

Furthermore, we all have a responsibility to persistently align our confessions with the Word of God by faith, to believe God for divine provision by faith, as well as to reign in life, walking in constant dominion over sin and the forces of darkness by faith. Indeed, everything we do in serving God and mankind is by personal faith, "for whatever *is* not from faith is sin" (*Romans 14:23*). The Christian life is a life lived righteously by personal faith in the Lord, in His Word, and in His sovereign power.

(8) It takes your personal choice to develop and operate personal faith

> But without faith *it is* impossible to please *Him,* for he who comes to God must believe that He is, and *that* He is a rewarder of those who diligently seek Him.
>
> *Hebrews 11:6*

We individually have the power to choose to come to God or reject Him; to hear His Word or refuse it; to believe His Word or disbelieve it; to apply His Word, which we believe, or to refuse to apply it; to please God or to displease Him. The choice is absolutely ours, but we must know that any choice we make in life has consequences; and some consequences, whether positive or negative, are eternal.

(9) To defeat Christians, the adversary primarily launches attacks on their personal faith

The devil attacks our personal faith to weaken or destroy it. Anywhere you find a backslidden or hopeless Christian, you have practically found a person whose personal faith has been successfully invaded and ruined by the adversary. When Satan plotted to sift Peter like wheat, his primary target was Peter's faith in the Lord; hence, Jesus alerted Peter that He had prayed for him, that his faith may not fail; and that, when he had returned to the Lord, he should strengthen his brethren (see *Luke 22:31-34*). This attack on the faith of Peter and the rest of the disciples happened when Jesus was arrested, tortured and brutalized. Peter denied him, while the rest of the disciples either deserted Him or watched him suffer from a distance. Peter and the other disciples were all restored to the Lord after the resurrection, except for Judas Iscariot, who betrayed Him and later committed suicide. The failure or lack of personal faith is what ultimately defeats a believer.

Box 6.1: Pause to actively pray these prayer pointers

1) My heavenly Father, give me the grace to commit myself to developing my faith in all the specific areas of my spiritual weakness, IJN.

2) I decree and declare that my faith shall neither fail, nor die, but will henceforth grow from strength to strength, IJN.

3) Lord, help me to invest more time and energy to listening to your Word, and studying to show myself approved before God as a diligent spiritual worker, IJN.

4) Lord, help me to be a faithful practitioner of your Word, IJN.

5) My heavenly Father, deliver me from the power of negative confessions that undermine the outcomes of my faith, IJN.

6) Lord, forgive me for all my negative confessions and, in your mercy, wash me by the Blood of Jesus, IJN.

7) I command all the barriers and limitations to my progress, which were imposed or reinforced by the words of my mouth, to be lifted, IJN.

8) I command all satanic attacks launched against my mind and faith to be shattered now, IJN.

9) I cast down all contrary imaginations and take captive every thought in my mind that exalts itself above the Word of God, IJN.

10) I command every satanic oracle and evil association working against my life and family to be broken in pieces, IJN.

11) Lord, give me the grace to change all my undesirable circumstances, by the power of my renewed faith in your Word, IJN.

12) Lord, thank you for answering my prayers today, IJN.

Chapter 7

Varying Measures of Faith

The Bible identifies two contrasting types of faith that are worth highlighting in this chapter: "counterfeit faith" and "genuine faith". "Counterfeit faith" is the term used in *2 Timothy 3:8* (NLT and RSV versions) to characterize the warped faith of people with depraved minds who oppose the truth of the Word of God. In today's world, there are many such people, and we must be careful to avoid them if we cannot convert them. Among them are some whose faith is founded on false religions, or what the Bible calls "doctrines of demons" (*1 Timothy 4:1*). They are prepared to die or kill others lawlessly for their faith. And when they kill the righteous, as Jesus remarked, they would think they are offering a holy service to God. It was such religious zealots who crucified Jesus—men of counterfeit faith who had no idea that their faith was wrongly founded on some form of satanic deception.

The term "genuine faith" is used in *2 Timothy 1:5* to describe the authentic faith, founded on the Holy Scriptures, which the young Timothy inherited from his godly grandmother Lois and mother Eunice. Genuine faith is what every Christian needs. You need to have an abundant measure of genuine faith in God's Word to be able to discern or recognize counterfeit faith. Every born-again child of God has a measure of genuine faith. Apostle Paul tells believers that God has given each of us "a measure of faith" (*Romans 12:3*), which should humble every beneficiary and make us think of ourselves with sober judgment, avoiding every possible tendency to be puffed up. This implies that we don't all have an equal level of faith but varying measures of faith, and each person should humbly treat whatever measure of faith they have as a "gift" from God.

Does this make our faith to be entirely God's responsibility? Absolutely not. We individually have a daily responsibility to invest in growing "the measure of faith" we received before or at the point of salvation through believing and obeying the Word of God (both *logos* and *rhema*) and through investing in hearing, understanding and doing "the word of faith" preached to us. We know from the Bible that our faith is designed to grow and could "grow exceedingly", like the faith of the brethren in Thessalonica (*2 Thessalonians 1:3*). God has not put any limit on the level to which anyone's faith could grow. There is always room for improvement and advancement till we transit to the other side of eternity to be with the Lord. Ultimately, it is only then that we will all "come to such unity in our faith… that we will be mature in the Lord, measuring up to the full and complete standard of Christ" (*Ephesians 4:13, NLT*).

We may not always know "the measure of faith" God has given to anybody or to us individually. Some faith preachers assert that God gives to all Christians an equal measure of faith at the point of redemption. In my view, the judgment about "the measure of faith" individually gifted to believers should be left to God. However, it is our individual responsibility to ensure that we persistently nurture whatever measure of faith we have received. The Bible identifies varying measures of faith exhibited by various people under diverse circumstances. Let me summarize them as follows:

(i) **Little Faith**—*the faith of Jesus' disciples during the stormy boat journey*

A person of little faith is one who may have been a believer for perhaps a couple of years but still has the faith level of a baby in the Lord. This is unacceptable, which was why Jesus rebuked His disciples while they were in their boat during a storm at sea. They exhibited little faith at a time when He expected their faith to have grown substantially because of all the words of God He had taught them and the miracles they had seen Him perform.

> But He [Jesus] said to them, "Why are you fearful, O you of little faith?" Then He arose and rebuked the winds and the sea, and there was a great calm.
>
> *Matthew 8:26*

Little faith causes you to see only with your natural eyes and not your spiritual eyes, and to become fearful when confronted with the pressing problems of daily life. Examples: when a believer has already been given authority by the Lord over all the powers of the enemy, but he sees an apparition of a familiar spirit in his home and runs away from his own house; when a threatening spirit appears to you in a dream and you wake up petrified, seeking prayer everywhere; when a Satan worshipper threatens to magically harm you, and you succumb to endless fear; when you wake up with a piercing pain in your chest and start imagining you have all sorts of incurable diseases; when you are diagnosed with an incurable disease and, out of fear, you immediately start preparing for your death and funeral, and so forth.

Sometimes a Christian could exhibit tendencies of negative or little faith in many areas but positive faith in just one aspect of life. For instance, he could have little or no faith in a miraculous healing when diagnosed with cancer, and similarly negative faith in overcoming marital storms; but at the same time, he could show great faith in pursuing financial breakthroughs. When the jobs of folks with little faith are under threat by a malicious boss, they can fast and pray for several days to overcome the obstacle or until they prevail. They could also take a similar positive faith initiative towards attending numerous interviews for a new and highly-paying job, even seeking an anointed servant of God to agree with them in prayer. What they don't realize is that, if only they would spiritually "fight" the negative medical report and the wicked stranger, for instance, behind their marital storms, in the same way they have fought to save their job or get a better job, they would likely get the same positive results.

Over the years, I have tried to counsel several Christians exhibiting this sort of markedly varied measures of faith when dealing with different problems, but most hardly get it. I recall a Christian lady who was facing multiple challenges regarding her job, marriage, and the struggles of her straying children. She was only interested in getting her children on the right track and saving her job, but not her marriage. This woman and her husband came to salvation many years before I did. She was referred to me for counselling and prayer, and I regularly spoke to her and prayed with her for more than two years, between 2016 and 2018.

By God's grace, our prayers progressively achieved the results she desired, results concerning her job and children; but all my efforts to encourage her to extend the same faith to save her marriage failed. I was full of empathy and far more zealous than she was to save her marriage. She repeatedly shared with me the various heartwarming dreams she was having about her marriage being restored and her estranged husband returning joyously to their matrimonial home, but she refused to pray for it to happen. She told me that she would be pleased to have her husband back but insisted that I had to intercede alone for that to happen because it was of lesser priority and possibility (in her reckoning) than saving her job and children. Unfortunately, this was not the only time I have witnessed such a fatalistic attitude from a client.

When you have already developed functional faith that secures miracles or answers in one area of life, God expects you to do the same thing and extend the same faith to other areas of life, where you could be facing practical challenges. Don't easily surrender to the enemy when he has stolen a valuable thing you still desire; don't feel that it is not a worthy prayer priority for you. It requires an actively renewed mind that thinks positively, prays positively, and acts positively with the help of the Holy Spirit to prevail in faith; and to prevail comprehensively, not in isolated patches. We also need to prevail in faith sustainably, not conceding any ground to the enemy.

Put in another way, positive thinking—a "can do" attitude of optimism and hope based on the confidence we have in the Word of God and our partnership with Him—are essential ingredients of prevailing faith. The American Protestant minister Norman Vincent Peale focused his highly inspirational *New York Times* bestseller, *The Power of Positive Thinking* (first published in 1952) on this important biblical faith principle of having an optimistic attitude to daily life based on the power of actively changed thoughts or positive thinking. Peale's influential book, one of the top twenty all-time best motivational books, is used extensively in *Positive Psychology* and many other secular fields to "show people that the roots of success lie in the mind and teach you how to believe in yourself, break the habit of worrying, and take control of your life by taking control of your thoughts and changing your attitude."[30]

Barak Obama's "Yes We Can" slogan, that inspired millions of Americans during his successful 2008 campaign to be elected as the first African-American President of the United States, is a tribute to what people can achieve through the enduring power of faith, hope, and positive thinking. As Caleb demonstrated in *Numbers 14:6-9*, the spirit of faith demands that one should not take sides with those who always see insurmountable giants and obstacles in positive and potentially impactful projects. For we walk by faith in God's Word and not by sight. By faith in God's spoken word through Moses, Caleb rejected the negative evil report of the ten spies with whom he went on a mission to spy out the Promised Land, and he quieted the disheartened people before Moses saying, "Let us go up at once and take possession, for we are well able to overcome it [*whatever challenges stood in the way of their taking the Promised Land*]" (*Numbers 13:30*).

(ii) **Little Faith versus Small Faith**—*the inability of the disciples of Jesus to heal the boy with the spirit of epilepsy*
Jesus attributed His disciples' inability to heal the troubled boy to their "little faith" but went on to say that, if they had faith as small as a mustard seed ("small faith"), they could move mountains with it.

> Jesus replied, "Oh, you stubborn, faithless people! How long shall I bear with you? Bring him here to me." Then Jesus rebuked the demon in the boy and it left him, and from that moment the boy was well.
>
> Afterwards the disciples asked Jesus privately, "Why couldn't we cast that demon out?"
>
> "**Because of your little faith**," Jesus told them. "For if you had **faith even as small as a tiny mustard seed**, you could say to this mountain, 'Move!' and it would go far away. Nothing would be impossible."
>
> *Matthew 17:17-20, TLB*

I have already explained "little faith" in the preceding section and therefore do not need to revisit it. "Small faith" is the level of faith of most young believers (not all) who may not know much of the Word of God and may not have had any remarkable divine encounters; however, their tiny bit of faith can accomplish great miracles if they put it to practical use. The small faith of a recently born-again Christian can move big mountains, but usually for a limited season. After the limited "honeymoon" period, God expects new believers to take all the necessary steps towards growing their faith through sound spiritual training and exercise, because increasingly they would require a greater and stronger measure of faith to move big mountains.

(iii) **Weak Faith versus Strong Faith**—*the choice Abraham made while waiting for God's promise for 25 years*

Faith, as I observed earlier, is an informed choice. What informs one's choice (in making any faith decision) matters. Is it personal ego, fear or concern about what people could say, doubt or fear that the Word of God might not "work", past experiences of disappointment, or a friend's contrary counsel? Or is it, most appropriately, an unwavering commitment to the prompting of the Holy Spirit, in accordance with the Word of God? Weak faith and strong faith are contrasting choices put before anybody confronted with a prolonged problem or spiritual battle. When faced with the two options, Abraham made the wise choice, and God credited it to him as righteousness.

> **And being not weak in faith**, he [Abraham] considered not his own body now dead, when he was about an hundred years old, neither yet the deadness of Sarah's womb: He staggered not at the promise of God through unbelief; **but was strong in faith**, giving glory to God; And being fully persuaded that, what he had promised, he was able also to perform.
>
> *Romans 4:19-21, KJV*

Our faith can be weakened when it is stretched or stressed over a long time by unmet expectations or prolonged challenges; or when we stop looking at the Word of God and His promises and start looking at the size and longevity of our problem. This is why it is important for believers to always encourage and pray for one another, regardless of how long anyone has been in the Lord. It wasn't because he was a novice or young believer that Elijah became discouraged when Jezebel threatened to kill him (after his victory at Mount Carmel over the prophets of Baal). Similarly with John the Baptist, the forerunner of Jesus Christ, who prophetically bore public testimony to the manifestation of the Christ as Messiah: he later doubted if Jesus was the Christ, during a low point of discouragement when Herod Antipas, the tetrarch of Galilee, imprisoned him for openly criticizing his (Herod's) unlawful marriage to his brother Philip's wife. Anyone can get discouraged or frustrated when undergoing difficult circumstances, but for the grace of God.

Strong faith, on the other hand, is the faith that has been stretched and tested by big problems, without being conquered or weakened. As is evident from *Romans 4:19-21* above, this was the type of faith demonstrated by Abraham, an unconquerable faith in God that stood a test of 25 years.

(iv) **Great Faith**—*the Centurion who sought healing for his servant*
Great faith is the faith that believes God for a great miracle against all odds. A good example could be when a sick person with a seemingly hopeless medical diagnosis decides to attend a major interdenominational crusade to listen to a highly-anointed guest minister, believing that God must heal him at the meeting. The miracle may or may not happen, but the person will not see any unexpected outcome as implying that his faith has failed. It simply means that God has not chosen to perform or manifest the miracle on that occasion, for whatever reason. More often than not, great faith will secure the expected result.

> The centurion answered and said, "Lord, I am not worthy that You should come under my roof. But only speak a word, and my servant will be healed. For I also am a man under authority, having soldiers under me. And I say to this *one*, 'Go,' and he goes; and to another, 'Come,' and he comes; and to my servant, 'Do this,' and he does *it*."

When Jesus heard *it,* He marveled, and said to those who followed, "**Assuredly, I say to you, I have not found such great faith, not even in Israel!**" And I say to you that many will come from east and west, and sit down with Abraham, Isaac, and Jacob in the kingdom of heaven. But the sons of the kingdom will be cast out into outer darkness. There will be weeping and gnashing of teeth."

Matthew 8:8-12

It is striking to note that the Centurion whom Jesus credited with such great faith in the above passage was an unbeliever or Gentile (by the classification of those days). That was why Jesus contrasted his extraordinary faith with the unbelief and unfaithfulness demonstrated by the sons of the kingdom.

(v) **Violent Faith—***the faith of the four men who removed the roof above Jesus to let down the paralytic where He was preaching*
You will not find the term "violent faith" in the Bible but, in one of His sermons, Jesus told His disciples that "from the days of John the Baptist until now the kingdom of heaven has suffered violence, and men of violence take it by force" (*Matthew 11:12, RSV*), implying they took it by "violent faith". I use the term "violent faith" to define a radical faith that defies all obstacles in order to provoke divine attention and secure desired results.

One of the best examples of violent faith in the Bible is the case of the four men who were carrying a paralytic to a meeting where Jesus was ministering, but they could not gain normal doorway access into the venue because of the overwhelming crowd. So, they climbed up to the roof and made an opening in it; from there, they let down the pallet on which the paralytic lay, lowering him until he was right in front of Jesus. Their strategy was spontaneous, costly and risky, but it worked.

"When Jesus saw their faith" (*Mark 2:5*), He first forgave the sins of the paralyzed man; but when He perceived in His spirit that some of the scribes were questioning in their hearts His authority to forgive sins, Jesus went a step further to heal the man by His spoken words.

Varying Measures of Faith

In narrating this spectacular healing miracle, reported in *Mark 2:1-12*, the Amplified Bible qualifies the faith of the four men who let down the paralytic through the roof as "active faith".

Beyond the aforementioned measures of faith, some other qualifiers used to describe and differentiate patterns of faith in the New Testament include "sincere faith" in *1 Timothy 1:5*, "shipwrecked faith" in *1 Timothy 1:19*, "rich faith" in *James 2:5*, "active faith" in *James 2:22* (*RSV*), and "overcoming faith" in *1 John 5:4*.

Finally, as Hagin (2017) teaches, based on *2 Peter 1:5-11*, faith is not meant to be an isolated spiritual force working by itself, but one that must work in conjunction with other spiritual forces, namely: diligence, virtue, knowledge, temperance, patience, godliness, kindness and love. Adding these complementary scriptural qualities will help to strengthen the effectiveness and outcomes of our faith.

Box 7.1: Pause to actively pray these prayer pointers

1) My heavenly Father, help me to pursue the knowledge of God's Word and to grow steadily in faith and spiritual wisdom, IJN.

2) Lord, help my mind not to be troubled but to find grace and peace in your Word, IJN.

3) Lord, give me the grace to find comfort and encouragement through the application of your Word, IJN.

4) Lord, help me not to be worried by negative things that you alone can handle in my life and family, IJN.

5) I decree and declare that I shall not be put to shame in this land, because I have put my trust in the Lord, IJN.

6) Lord, assign your angels to arrest and overthrow every agent of darkness who has been permitted in the spiritual realm to afflict me and my family, IJN.

7) I command every fire of affliction that I and my family have been experiencing to end now, IJN.

8) By the power in the Blood of Redemption, I command every water of tribulation that has flooded my life and family to end, with immediate effect, IJN.

9) Lord, help me to henceforth walk into new opportunities, open doors, divine contacts, and supernatural favours, IJN.

10) By the mercies in the Blood of Redemption, I declare that the Lord will bless the works of my hands and keep me in good health, IJN.

11) Lord, help me to be faithful to you in all things and to be committed to serving you with all my heart, IJN.

> "And blessed is she that believed: for there shall be a performance of those things which were told her from the Lord" (*Luke 1:45, KJV*).

12) By my renewed faith in God's Word, I declare that the Lord is watching over every due or overdue prophecy or revelation issued concerning me, to perform them speedily, IJN.

Chapter 8

Heroes in the Bible and Their Works of Personal Faith

"Now faith is the substance of things hoped for, the evidence of things not seen. For by it the elders obtained a good testimony. By faith we understand that the worlds were framed by the word of God, so that the things which are seen were not made of things which are visible."

Hebrews 11:1-3

It is remarkable that, by their lifestyle and the application of their "measure of faith" or personal faith, the elders of old, who have gone ahead of us to eternity, obtained a good testimony and divine approval. The entire Hebrews 11 is full of the works of men and women who applied their personal faith to please God, achieve victories, and fulfil destinies. By studying what the heroes in the Bible achieved through the application of their faith, we will learn more about the multi-dimensional components and purposes of personal faith in the service of God.

(1) Excellent and acceptable sacrifices

By faith—personal faith—Abel offered an excellent and acceptable sacrifice to God (*Hebrews 11:4*). And God offered a priceless and excellent sacrifice of and to Himself, in order to redeem us from our sins. It is faith and love that make a sacrifice excellent before God. Serving God demands daily sacrifices, and some excellent sacrifices we are required to make by faith can be inconvenient and costly. Jesus loved us to the point of sacrificing His life for our sins, according to God's will, to satisfy the righteous demands of divine justice. What excellent sacrifice can you make, in appreciation of God's love for you, and to honour Him?

(2) Living to please God

By faith, Enoch lived in a way that pleased God (*Hebrews 11:5*). It takes faith in God and the fear of God to consistently live a life that pleases Him, especially in an adulterous and sinful generation when so many people live lawlessly and prosper in it, apparently without any foreseeable consequences—from the sinner's viewpoint, at least. Enoch lived for 365 years in an exceedingly sinful generation and consistently pleased God by faith (*Genesis 5:21-24*). The outcome of his faith was that God took him by supernatural transition and he did not experience death. We must live to obey and please God; this is the whole duty of man, according to *Ecclesiastes 12:13-14*.

(3) Obedience to divine warning

By faith, Noah obeyed God and built a gigantic ark (*Hebrews 11:7*). Noah walked in godly fear and heeded divine warning in a highly corrupt and violent generation. It takes great faith to walk with God in a generation like Noah's (*Genesis 6:9-14*). The outcome of Noah's faith was the protection of the remnant of eight (Noah and his family), through whom humanity was preserved and perpetuated.

(4) Obedience to divine command without counting the cost and in spite of foreseeable risks

By his personal faith, Abraham left Ur in Chaldea at God's calling and went out, not knowing where he was going (*Hebrews 11:8*). It takes great faith to obey God, as Abraham did, venturing out with his entire household on a high-risk relocation to an unknown land in a far country (*Genesis 12:1-6*). Sometimes a step of faith could be a risky adventure and, all too often, be inconvenient and costly, at least from a human point of view. But God honoured Abraham for his faith and fulfilled all His promises to him, making him the father of many nations and a channel of divine blessings for all those in every generation who would live by faith as children of God.

(5) Waiting and receiving divine promises

Hebrews 11:11 reports that, by her personal faith, Sarah received the power to conceive, and she bore Isaac in her old age. But we know that she waited a long time—about 25 years—before this promise was fulfilled (see *Genesis 17:15-19*). Waiting to receive God's promises can sometimes be a long and challenging process; as such, many Christians do not have the "stomach" for it. However, patience is a necessary component of faith because the Bible instructs us that those who believe in the Lord shall not make haste. Moreover, we are urged not to become spiritually sluggish, but rather to imitate those who, through faith and patience, inherit the promises of God (*Hebrews 6:12*).

(6) Obedience in doing the seemingly impossible

By his personal faith, Abraham was willing to offer up Isaac, his "only begotten son," trusting that God would be able to raise him up (*Hebrews 11:17-19*). Our faith in God can be tested by seemingly impossible circumstances, sometimes without our knowing that it is all a test of faith. God resolved to test Abraham's faith, but Abraham did not know it was a test. He was simply determined to obey God unconditionally, and in all circumstances (see *Genesis 22:1-17*). Abraham's faith was tested almost to a breaking point, and he passed the test by demonstrating his commitment to unconditional obedience to God. Every believer's faith in God will be tested by diverse trials. We all need grace to pass every test of faith.

(7) Bequeathing covenant blessings to the next generation

By his personal faith, Isaac blessed his sons, Jacob and Esau, and prophetically exhorted them concerning things of the future (*Hebrews 11:20*). Most likely, Isaac exhorted his two sons to follow and obey the Lord, so that it would be well with them; I imagine he could not have taught them otherwise. We have not truly succeeded as children of God if God's covenant is not perpetuated beyond our generation. We must pass on God's covenant blessings to our children and the next generation, exhorting them to obey the Lord. If previous generations had not perpetuated the new covenant in Christ to us, we would all have been lost and the kingdom of darkness could have overrun the entire world. Our generation *shall* win the battle over the faith and future of our children; we shall not lose to the devil, and likewise our children, IJN.

(8) Defying ungodly decrees by governing authorities

Faith in God can sometimes bring one into collision with governing authorities. *Hebrews 11:23* states that, by faith, Moses' parents refused to carry out Pharaoh's command to kill their male child, not minding the punishment for their defiance—which could have possibly been the execution of both the parents and their son (*Exodus 1:22; 2:1-4*). Apparently, most of the Israelites could have carried out this ungodly command for fear of the consequences of disobedience.

Daniel, Shadrach, Meshach and Abednego on different occasions encountered ungodly decrees, which they victoriously defied by faith during the seventy years when many Israelites were exiled to Babylon. May the Lord give us the courage to stand conscientiously in defence of the gospel of His grace at all times, IJN.

(9) Forsaking temporal pleasures and benefits to please God

All too often, faith could thrust us into circumstances where we may have to choose between fleeting pleasures and standing for God; between playing along with popular culture and identifying with the cross of Christ. According to *Hebrews 11:24-29,* Moses turned his back on the fleeting pleasures of sin and sided with the downtrodden children of Israel, ultimately leading them out of Egypt and obediently carrying out the difficult commands of God.

It is not a convenient stance to take, but personal faith sometimes requires us to do what may be inconvenient and make tough decisions to please God.

(10) Overcoming difficult obstacles

You need great personal faith to surmount difficult obstacles and impossible mountains. *Hebrews 11:30* exhorts us thus: "By faith the walls of Jericho fell down after they were encircled for seven days." Jericho was a highly fortified city, but the children of Israel conquered it by faithfully following some divine commands that did not make any battlefield sense (*Joshua 6:1-5; 20-22*).

Sometimes God's strategy or solution to a difficult problem may not make natural sense, but it works when one executes it by faith.

(11) Exemption from mass destruction

Acting on your personal faith in God and living by faith can preserve your life and exempt you and your household from any acts of mass destruction permitted by God. Rahab believed in the power of God and helped to hide the Israelite spies who had been sent to Jericho (*Hebrews 11:31*). Her act of faith saved her and her loved ones from perishing together with all the people of Jericho who did not believe that God had given their land to the Israelites. May the Lord place immense value on your life and exempt you and your household from any destruction He permits on earth at any time, IJN.

(12) Surviving life-threatening storms

Personal faith does not insulate us from the storms of life, but it does equip us to withstand and overcome them. In fact, "storms *and strains* in life are not meant to break us but to bend us towards God *through faith.*"[31] According to *Hebrews 11:32-38*, many of the Old Testament heroes of faith—people like Gideon, Barak, Samson, Jephthah, David Samuel, and the prophets—trusted God to give them courage, endurance, resilience and victory. They refused to compromise their faith in God, even in the midst of life-threatening storms. Their lives and the outcomes of their faith are examples to us in this generation, inspiring us to fight the good fight of faith, that we might ultimately take hold of eternal life, to which we have been called.

Box 8.1: Pause to actively pray these prayer pointers

1) My heavenly Father, help me to obtain good testimonies by my faith, IJN.
2) Lord, help me to live by faith in your Word and only in ways that are pleasing to you, IJN.
3) My heavenly Father, deliver me from self-centeredness and help me to use my faith to serve God and humanity, IJN.
4) Lord, help me to prioritize the need to apply my faith to offering excellent and acceptable sacrifices to God, IJN.

Box 8.2: Pause to actively pray these prayer pointers

5) My heavenly Father, help me to be sensitive to divine warnings through the ministry of the indwelling Holy Spirit, IJN.

6) Lord, may you show mercy to the land of my habitation and forgive our sins and the trespasses of our leaders, IJN.

7) My heavenly Father, may you spare our land from your wrath and judgment, IJN.

8) My heavenly Father, may you heal our land by the mercies in the Blood of redemption and the ministry of your gospel of salvation, IJN.

9) I command every permission obtained by the adversary to bring calamity upon our land to be nullified by the mercies in the Blood of redemption, IJN.

10) Lord Jesus, may you strengthen your church—the body of Christ—in our land, by the revelation of your Word and in all spiritual power and boldness, IJN.

11) By the mercies in the Blood of redemption, I make a case of exemption from pestilence and premature death for all the members of my household and local church, IJN.

12) My heavenly Father, help me to be unconditionally committed to obeying your Word by faith, IJN.

13) Lord, give me the grace to reject the fleeting pleasures of sin by a faithful commitment to your superior ways, IJN.

14) I shall not die but live to fulfil my destiny and proclaim the good works of the Lord, IJN.

15) God of all grace, may you make all grace available to me from today to fulfil my calling and ministry in the Lord, IJN.

16) Lord, thank you for answering my prayers today, IJN.

PART 3

ADDITIONAL PRAYERS FOR DIVERSE PURPOSES AND NEEDS

The prayers listed below can be modified to suit one's special circumstances and needs

A. **Taking Personal Responsibility for Outcomes of My life**
   (*Judges 11:1-11; Isaiah 41:10; Ezekiel 18:20-24; 2 Corinthians 5:17; Philippians 4:13*)

   1) My heavenly Father, please give me the grace to take personal responsibility for all the negative outcomes of my life and to avoid blaming others, IJN.

   2) Lord, forgive me for hurting others (name the persons) and causing (through my words or actions) any negative outcomes in their lives, IJN.

   3) My heavenly Father, give me the grace to forgive all those whom Satan has used to hurt and afflict me, IJN.

   4) By the Lord's mantle of fire, I break loose from every ungodly habit and lifestyle, IJN.

   5) Strongholds of ungodly distraction in my life, be uprooted and destroyed by fire, IJN.

   6) I command the fire of God to destroy all the inherited spiritual yokes and chains of the enemy in my life, IJN.

   7) By the power in the Blood of redemption, I break away from all the consequences of the transgressions and spiritual transactions of my father's house, IJN.

   8) By the power in the Blood of redemption, I break away from all the consequences of the transgressions and spiritual transactions of my mother's house, IJN.

   9) Lord, help me to make the fear of God a consuming passion within me, IJN.

   10) By the power in the Blood of redemption, I break every power of addiction to sinful habits and lifestyle, IJN.

   11) I believe and declare that I can do all things through Christ who strengthens me, IJN.

12) I command all messengers of Satan sponsoring blackmail and stagnation against me to scatter by fire, IJN.

13) My heavenly Father, please give me divine wisdom and power to correct and rebuild my life, IJN.

14) Let the power of the Holy Ghost overshadow and guide me to achieve His divine purpose, IJN.

15) I command the terrifying fire of the living God upon all the forces of darkness sponsoring false dreams to manipulate the answers to my prayers, IJN.

16) My heavenly Father, I claim an unhindered and timely delivery of every good thing that has been given to me by your sovereign power, IJN.

17) Lord, raise a voice for me in important places where my case is being decided behind closed doors, IJN.

18) I appropriate the power in the Blood of Jesus to mend my ways, renew my thoughts, and walk in a newness of life, IJN.

19) My heavenly Father, help me to increase my passion for hearing, studying, understanding, believing in, and obeying your Word, IJN.

B. **Deliverance from the Powers of Darkness and Breaking the Dominion of Sin** (*Job 1:8-12; Daniel 2:20-22; Psalm 7:9, KJV; Luke 22:31-34; Romans 6:14-19*)

1) Lord, I thank you for all your goodness; I am grateful for your protection and provision, IJN.

2) Lord, wherever I have surrendered to the dominion of sin, may you forgive and restore me to prevailing grace, IJN.

3) I break the power of submission and slavery to sinful passions over my life, IJN.

4) By the power in the Blood of redemption, I break the stronghold of bitterness and anger in my life, IJN.

5) By the power in the Blood of redemption, I revolt against vulnerability to the spirit of provocation and offence, IJN.

6) By the power of the Holy Spirit, I cut off every contrary power manipulating my thoughts and decisions, IJN.

Additional Prayers for Diverse Purposes and Needs

7) Lord, deliver me today from every destruction that sin has caused in my life and destiny, IJN.

8) By the power in the Blood of Jesus, I command the yokes of sin and death to be broken over my life and household, IJN.

9) I declare that sin shall no longer have dominion over me, since I am not under the law of sin, IJN.

10) Lord, let the power and grace to defeat every sinful habit overshadow me now, IJN.

11) Lord, give me the grace to walk in complete obedience to your Word and deliver me from the error of intentional sins, IJN.

12) Lord, by your divine power, I command a push-back to the storms of sin and darkness released against your church in this land, IJN.

13) Arrows of distress, insomnia and depression fired into my life, I command you to scatter and return to your senders, IJN.

14) Curses of failure and demotion fired against my life, I command you to scatter and return to your senders, IJN.

15) I command every satanic bargain in the spiritual realm, that has given the enemy permission to attack me and my family, to scatter by fire, IJN.

16) I command every satanic bargain in the spiritual realm, that has given the enemy permission to attack my church and ministry, to scatter by the power in the Blood of redemption, IJN.

17) By the power in the Blood of Jesus, I overrule and disallow all satanic warrant officers assigned in the spiritual realm to confiscate my treasures and blessings, IJN.

18) I terminate every satanic warrant issued to arrest or reverse my breakthroughs, IJN.

19) Lord, send your warring angels to re-open every good door the enemy has closed against your church in this land, IJN.

20) I decree by divine authority, let every wickedness of the wicked that has held back my life come to an end right now, IJN.

21) I decree by divine authority, let every wickedness of the wicked resisting the great doors of increase opened to the church of Jesus Christ in this land come to an end, IJN.

22) I command all evil winds of contamination and setback released against our ministry to scatter and return to their senders, IJN.

23) I command all evil winds of chaos and confusion released against me and my family to scatter and return to their senders, IJN.

24) Lord, release upon us the grace to enjoy the blessings of the new covenant, blessings of goodness and favour, IJN.

C. **Walking in the Blessings of the Tribe of Asher: the Blessings of the Most Blessed** *(Deuteronomy 33:24)*

1) My heavenly Father, may you bestow on me the peculiar blessing pronounced on the tribe of Asher: the blessing of the most blessed, and the favour of the most favoured among many, IJN.

2) Let the peculiar blessing pronounced on the tribe of Asher distinguish all the students in our church with excellent performance in their studies, IJN.

3) Let the peculiar blessing and favour of the tribe of Asher establish the marital destiny of all those desiring to marry in our ministry in this year, IJN.

4) Let the peculiar blessing and favour of the tribe of Asher prosper every business in our ministry from today, moving forward, IJN.

5) Lord, establish me in supernaturally endowed wealth from this year, moving forward, IJN.

6) By the power in the Blood of redemption, I dip my feet in the Lord's anointing oil for sanctification and favour, IJN.

7) Lord, may you increase in me the power, wisdom and opportunity to get wealth, IJN.

8) Lord, may you release your favour upon all immigration cases and resident permit, citizenship and visa applications in our ministry, IJN.

9) I command every judgment passed against me by the kingdom of darkness to be cancelled and reversed, IJN.

10) My heavenly Father, may you frustrate the conspiracies and devices of the wicked against my life and family, IJN.

Additional Prayers for Diverse Purposes and Needs

11) I command every human agent resisting my divinely assigned position and destiny to be disappointed and disgraced, IJN.

12) I declare that my feet are supernaturally anointed; therefore, from today, moving forward, my feet will carry me to persons, places and positions of favour and good news, IJN.

D. Claiming New Open Doors for Restoration of Fortunes
(2 Kings 8:1-8; Jeremiah 30:18-22; John 1:16)

1) Lord, may you open to the body of Christ new doors for the harvest of souls in this land, IJN.

2) My heavenly Father, may you open to the body of Christ new doors for deliverance of the oppressed in this land, IJN.

3) My heavenly Father, may you open to the body of Christ new doors for the ministry of the needy in this land, IJN.

4) I decree that my days and years of stagnation and famine are over, IJN.

5) Lord, by your divine arrangement, help me not to be wrongly located away from my place of blessing at any time, IJN.

6) Lord, help me to appear at the right place and at the right time for my fortunes to be established, IJN.

7) Lord, raise a victorious voice for me in every place where my case comes under deliberation in this year, IJN.

8) I receive grace from the Lord to cut off myself from every disappointment and setback of the past, IJN.

9) I command any hidden evil covenant working against my progress to be terminated, IJN.

10) My heavenly Father, may you enlist me among those you have set aside for uncommon blessings in this season, IJN.

E. Claiming New Open Doors for Double Restoration
(Job 42:10-12; Isaiah 40:1-2; Revelation 3:7)

1) Lord, may you open to the body of Christ new doors for soul-winning and the work of ministry in this land, IJN.

2) My heavenly Father, send your warring angels to open every good door that the enemy has closed against me and my household, IJN.

3) By the consuming fire of the Holy Ghost, I command a reopening of every good door the enemy has closed in my life, against the will of God, IJN.

4) By the mercies in the Blood of Jesus, I decree and command a double restoration of every good door the enemy has recently closed in my life, IJN.

5) Multiple doors of the "power to get wealth", locate me today by fire, IJN.

6) Lord, give me the grace and wisdom to be a good manager of relationships you have divinely arranged in my favour, IJN.

7) Lord, give me the courage and grace to break away from every relationship that works against my destiny and spiritual growth, IJN.

8) Lord, help me to recognize and strengthen every relationship that enhances my divine destiny, IJN.

9) Lord, help me to recognize and strengthen every relationship that could enable me to make a positive impact on the destinies of others, IJN.

10) Lord, lead me to establish new relationships through which I could extend the love of God to others, IJN.

11) By the mercies in the Blood of Jesus, I command new doors of relationships of destiny to open in my favour, IJN.

12) God of double restoration, remember me today and let this month be my special month of divine visitation, IJN.

F. **Open Doors for God's Word and for Us** *(Colossians 4:2-6; 1 Corinthians 16:8-9; 2 Kings 7:1-8; Revelation 3:7-8)*

1) Lord, we thank you for the open doors for the work of ministry that you have set before us as a church, IJN.

2) Lord, may you continuously confirm your Word preached and taught in this land by miraculous signs and wonders, IJN.

3) My heavenly Father, may you open to us more doors for the effective work of ministry in this land, IJN.

4) I arrest and banish into the hottest pits of the desert all the spiritual adversaries blocking the divine open doors set before the body of Christ in this land, IJN.

Additional Prayers for Diverse Purposes and Needs

5) My heavenly Father, may you shake the spiritual foundations of this land to trigger a supernatural harvest of souls for your kingdom, IJN.

6) Lord, may you send more labourers and angelic forces for the harvest of souls in this land, IJN.

7) Lord, help me to henceforth encounter fresh opportunities to promote the cause of your kingdom, IJN.

8) Lord, open my eyes to see divine opportunities you have set before me in this season, IJN.

9) Lord, may you release upon me a special grace for the restoration of any destiny-changing opportunities I have lost in the past, IJN.

10) As the four Hebrew lepers became divine instruments to bring Elisha's prophetic words to manifestation, Lord, use me to fulfil a prophecy in someone's life and use others to fulfil prophecies in my life, IJN.

11) My heavenly Father, let me encounter unusual divine opportunities for breakthroughs in this season, IJN.

12) My heavenly Father, let the grace to rise above my present spiritual and financial levels locate me now, IJN.

13) My heavenly Father, let fresh opportunities to be a channel of blessing to others locate me now, IJN.

14) Lord, may you use me to be a problem-solver in the lives of many, IJN.

G. Resisting the Reproach of the Wicked Ruling over Us
(Joel 2:17, KJV; Proverbs 28:28; Proverbs 29:16)

1) By the power in the Blood of redemption, we refuse and reject the reproach of the wicked ruling over us; may they never be able to torment or oppress us in this land, IJN.

2) By divine authority, we resist every agent of spiritual wickedness aspiring to a position of power in this country; let their aspirations come to nothing, IJN.

3) We frustrate the rise of the wicked to positions of power and authority in this land, IJN.

4) My heavenly Father, silence and disgrace all agents of wickedness working against my progress in this land, IJN.

5) By the power in the Blood of redemption, I refuse and reject the reproach of the wicked lording it over me in any sphere of life, IJN.

6) By divine authority, I resist every messenger of darkness aspiring to a position of power and authority in my workplace; let their aspirations come to nothing, IJN.

7) I frustrate the rise of the wicked to positions of power and authority in our schools and workplaces, IJN.

8) Lord, assign your fighting angels to pull down all the wicked agents of darkness exacted upon us, IJN.

9) Lord, give our political leaders the wisdom and foresight to formulate good policies and govern well, IJN.

H. **Growing in Favour with God and with Men** *(Luke 2:52; Psalm 19:14; Romans 8:1-2; 14:16-18)*

1) My heavenly Father, renew your stamp of divine approval upon my life and help me to walk in obedience to your will, IJN.

2) Lord, give me the grace to serve you in righteousness, peace and joy in the Holy Ghost, IJN.

3) Lord, give me the grace to henceforth purify and align the meditations of my heart and words of my mouth in line with your holy scriptures, IJN.

4) I decree that the spirit of rejection shall no longer have any dominion over me; I break the hold of the spirit of rejection over my life, IJN.

5) By the authority of the Holy Spirit, I decree that I shall henceforth be accepted wherever the Lord opens a door of opportunity for me, IJN.

6) By the Lord's covenant of peace, I decree that I shall enjoy abundant peace of mind and peace in the land of my habitation, IJN.

7) Let the presence and power of the Lord in me henceforth terrify evil people into submission, IJN.

Additional Prayers for Diverse Purposes and Needs

8) Lord, may you put your stamp of approval on my prayers and cause the vessels you intend to use to bring forth the answers to manifest speedily, IJN.

9) Lord, by the power of your divine approval, vindicate me before all those who have plotted my downfall, IJN.

10) I decree that the promises of the Lord concerning my life shall no longer delay; let God arise and let all the forces of delay assigned against me scatter, IJN.

11) My heavenly Father, release a new grace of your favour upon me: favour with God and men, IJN.

I. Proclaiming a Highway of Victory from the Wilderness of Affliction *(Isaiah 40:3-5; Micah 2:1-3; Matthew 3:1-3)*

1. Lord, show mercy to me in every way I have gotten myself into the wilderness—whether through my transgressions, ignorance or folly, IJN.

2. I stretch forth my hands to the third heaven to receive grace to prevail in the wilderness of affliction; Lord, may you deliver me from every wilderness experience, IJN.

3. By the authority of the Living God, I frustrate all the evil devices of the wicked against me and my family; let their hands not be able to perform their wicked enterprises, IJN.

4. Lord, execute judgment against all those who stay awake at night, devising evil against me and my family, IJN.

5. I decree and declare that no human being has the power to keep me in the wilderness, because the Greater One lives in the inside of me, IJN.

6. I command all the satanic valleys fighting to prolong my wilderness experience to be lifted, IJN.

7. I command the valleys of depression, fear, anxiety, doubt and discouragement waging war against my soul to scatter, IJN.

8. I command every threatening mountain standing before me and my family to be levelled, IJN.

9. I break every chain of wilderness degradation fastened on any part of my body or destiny, IJN.

10. I decree and declare that I and my family are coming out of every wilderness experience better than we entered it, IJN.

11. By the mercies in the Blood of redemption, I command every wilderness experience to start working out a greater weight of glory, restoration and reward for me and my family, IJN.

12. By the power of the Living God, I pull myself out of the wilderness now, through the supernatural highway the Lord has made for my deliverance, IJN.

13. Lord, may you reveal your distinguishing glory upon the body of Christ in this land, IJN.

J. Destroying the Foundations of Demonic Dreams and Their Consequences *(Job 4:12-19; John 15:1-8)*

1. Lord, I thank you for all your blessings and miracles, IJN.

2. By the mercies in the Blood of redemption, I repent of all past and present sins and sinful lifestyle that have opened doors of demonic dreams in my life, IJN.

3. My heavenly Father, increase in me the spiritual capacity to understand dreams and to handle them prayerfully, IJN.

4. My heavenly Father, may you give me the grace and power to discern all diabolical spirits that manifest in my dreams and visions, IJN.

5. By the authority of the Holy Spirit, I destroy the demonic foundations of evil dreams in my life, and I break the covenants behind them, IJN.

6. By the power in the Blood of redemption, I destroy all inherited demonic transactions that expose me to evil dreams, IJN.

7. By the power in the Blood of redemption, I break the curse of demonic dreams and setbacks arising from all my previous ungodly relationships, IJN.

8. I command every demonic register and database holding evil charges, records and allegations against me to be destroyed by the fire of the Holy Ghost, IJN.

Additional Prayers for Diverse Purposes and Needs

9. By the power in the Blood of redemption, I command all infirmities, diseases and afflictions in my life that have their origin in demonic dreams, visions or apparitions to be destroyed, IJN.

10. My heavenly Father, manifest your glory in all areas of my life, IJN.

K. Breaking the Yokes of Poverty and Hardship
(Psalm 127:1-2; Proverbs 14:23; Isaiah 10:27; 30:19-21)

1. By the power in the Blood of redemption, I revoke every power of evil dedication over my life, IJN.

2. I command any contrary god contending for a place in my life to be disarmed and rendered impotent, IJN.

3. I command all evil powers pursuing me by reason of negative parental and ancestral covenants to scatter by fire, IJN.

4. I command all inherited yokes of poverty and hardship over my life and family to be shattered, IJN.

5. I command all wicked powers and evil gatherings that are monitoring my life to be terminated, IJN.

6. I command every dream of the night that fosters poverty or hardship in my life to scatter and be disannulled, IJN.

7. By the power in the Blood of redemption, I command every curse of darkness that exposes me and my household to the bread of sorrow and adversity to be nullified, IJN.

8. By the power in the Blood of redemption, I nullify every curse of dishonour and shame that has followed me from my father's house, IJN.

9. By the power in the Blood of redemption, I nullify every curse of poverty and hardship that has followed me from my father's house, IJN.

10. I command all the evil limitations that hindered the progress of my parents to be lifted off my life and my household, IJN.

11. I shall not labour in vain in any work that I do; Lord, deliver me from all fruitless enterprises and bless the works of my hands, IJN.

12. Lord, deploy your angels to watch over my family and all those under my prayer cover, IJN.

13. My heavenly Father, may you teach me and lead me in the way that I should henceforth walk to find abundant peace and prosperity, IJN.

L. **Grace for Prosperity** *(Genesis 39:2-4; 22-23, RSV; Malachi 3:8-12; 2 Corinthians 9:6-8)*

1. I command every recurrent hardship experience in my life to be terminated, IJN.

2. By the power in the Blood of redemption, I bind and dislodge all the poverty-sponsoring demonic entities manifesting in my dreams, IJN.

3. Lord, forgive me for all the ways I might have been unfaithful to you with the financial blessings you have given me, IJN.

4. Lord, deliver me from the error of stinginess and help me to be a passionate and cheerful giver from today, moving forward, IJN.

5. My heavenly Father, give me the grace to henceforth obey the command of the Lord Jesus Christ about laying for myself treasures in heaven where moths and rust do not corrupt and where thieves cannot break in to steal my treasures and rewards, IJN.

6. My heavenly Father, give me the grace to henceforth sow generously into the advancement of your kingdom here on earth, so that the spiritual law of abundant harvest will become more evident in my life, IJN.

7. Lord, help me to henceforth be a faithful steward of all the money you give me, to be faithful to you in my tithes and offerings, IJN.

8. Lord, protect my resources and family from the attacks of devourers, IJN.

9. My heavenly Father, release upon me today the grace that established and prospered Joseph in a strange land, IJN.

10. Let the Lord be magnified, who takes pleasure in my prosperity as His servant, IJN.

Additional Prayers for Diverse Purposes and Needs

M. **The Power to Prosper**
   (Matthew 6:33; Proverbs 8:18; 1 Kings 3:5-14, RSV; 3 John 1:2)

   1. Lord, multiply upon your church in this land the grace to diligently seek your kingdom and serve you passionately, IJN.

   2. Lord, multiply upon me the grace to diligently produce befitting works to advance your kingdom, IJN.

   3. My heavenly Father, let your grace for enduring wealth and honour be released upon your church in our community, IJN.

   4. Lord, release the grace that will prosper the righteous in our community, and let their prosperity multiply peace and joy in the land, IJN.

   5. My heavenly Father, as part of your prosperity agenda, overthrow the wicked from strategic positions in our land and let the righteous take their place, IJN.

   6. Lord, prosper me to be a channel of blessing to many, IJN.

   7. Lord, may you increase in me the spirit of wisdom and revelation necessary for all-round prosperity, IJN.

   8. Lord, may you bless the works of my hands and creative ideas of my mind, IJN.

   9. My heavenly Father, deliver me from any enterprise that does not have your divine approval, IJN.

   10. Lord, give me the grace to embark only on projects and business relationships that have your divine approval, from today moving forward, IJN.

   11. My heavenly Father, anoint me afresh today with the Holy Spirit and with power—let the anointing to be made whole and to make others whole fall graciously upon me, IJN.

   12. My heavenly Father, let the anointing of the Holy Spirit break every yoke preventing my healing and breakthroughs, IJN.

   13. Lord, let your yoke-breaking anointing root out everything in my past that is hindering my present life and preventing my moving forward, IJN.

   14. Lord, let your yoke-breaking anointing destroy every inherited curse in the foundation of my life that hinders my prosperity and progress, IJN.

15. Lord, deliver me from the wicked agendas of the enemy; I refuse to walk into any satanic agendas, IJN.

16. I receive grace to henceforth prosper in God's divine agenda for my life; and I command every contrary power interfering with this God-given grace to scatter by fire, IJN.

N. **Revoking All Known and Unknown Curses** *(Isaiah 49:24-25, KJV; Lamentations 5:7; 1 Chronicles 4:9-10; 2 Kings 2: 19-22; 1 John 3:8; Acts 10:38; Galatians 3:13-14)*

1) By the overriding power in the Blood of Jesus, I break every curse of lawful captivity (as promised in *Isaiah 49:24-25*[32]) and affliction over my life, IJN.

2) By the power in the Blood of Jesus, I terminate and renounce every covenant with the witchcraft altars of my community of origin, IJN.

3) By the power in the Blood of redemption, I command all the spoken and written curses suffered by my ancestors to be restrained from affecting my life, IJN.

4) I command all generational curses of evil afflicting my life and household to be disannulled, IJN.

5) By the mercies in the Blood of redemption, I claim divine exemption from all afflictions against me, springing from any legacy of abominable iniquities in my place of origin, IJN.

6) By the authority in the name of Jesus, I revoke every judicial sentence against me in the spiritual realm; I am discharged and acquitted, IJN.

7) By the power in the Blood of redemption, I claim divine acquittal from every inherited disease and destiny setback caused by the iniquities of my forefathers, IJN.

8) By the power in the Blood of redemption, I uproot and destroy every strange object, affliction or growth in my body planted by the evil one, IJN.

9) I command every contention for my life and destiny mounted by ancestral spirits to scatter by the power in the Blood of redemption, IJN.

10) By the power in the Blood of redemption, I revoke every curse of household wickedness and subversion operating against my life and family, IJN.

Additional Prayers for Diverse Purposes and Needs

11) By the power in the Blood of redemption, I break and reverse every unknown curse of public disgrace, setback or embarrassment working against my progress, IJN.

12) By the power in the Blood of redemption, I nullify every unknown curse of bitterness, barrenness or miscarriage hanging over my life and family, IJN.

13) By the power in the Blood of redemption, I decree and declare that no curse, known or unknown, is permitted to follow me from today, moving forward, IJN.

14) I decree and declare that from today, moving forward, the covenant blessings of Abraham shall follow me and my household, IJN.

15) Lord, thank you for answering all my prayers, IJN.

O. **Life Preservation by the Mercies of God** *(Psalm 79:11; Hebrews 9:27; Isaiah 54:15; Job 14:14; 2 Thessalonians 3:16; Proverbs 25:25; 1 Corinthians 15:57-58)*

1) By the mercies in the Blood of redemption, I command an end to every regime of calamity in my life and family, IJN.

2) By the mercies of the Living God, my life and household shall be preserved from destruction, according to the greatness of God's power, IJN.

3) By the power in the Blood of redemption, I break every appointment with death over my life and household, IJN.

4) I command every spirit of death appointed for me and members of my family and our local congregation to be swallowed up in victory, IJN.

5) I command every wicked gathering against me and my family to be broken in pieces, IJN.

6) Lord, change my life story for good, like I have never experienced previously, IJN.

7) Lord, may you give me, my family, and our local church uninterrupted peace always and by all means, IJN.

8) By the power in the Blood of redemption, I summon life-changing good news to locate me from far and near places, IJN.

9) By the mercies of the Living God, I shall be steadfast and immovable, always excelling in the work of the Lord, IJN.

10) I command divine victory to henceforth follow me in every good work I do, IJN.

11) Lord, lay your invisible hand upon me and my household for all-round favour and blessings, IJN.

P. **Grace to Forget All Former Misfortunes and Setbacks**
(Isaiah 43:18-19; 53:4-6; Nahum 1:9, KJV; Jeremiah 29:11; Philippians 3:12-16)

1) My heavenly Father, may you perform a supernatural surgery on my mind and heal me of all memories of grief, sorrow and trauma from any former disappointment or misfortune, IJN.

2) Lord, touch the hearts of members of my family and heal everyone of memories of grief, sorrow and trauma from any previous ordeals, IJN.

3) Lord Jesus, thank you because you have borne our griefs and sorrows; I cast all my depression, setbacks and disappointments at your feet because you care for me, IJN.

4) I break the power of past incidents of misfortune in my life, and I render them impotent, IJN.

5) I connect to the power of the new things the Lord is doing in my life, and I wait to receive them, IJN.

6) Lord, help me to learn every lesson that will make previous afflictions never repeat again in my life, IJN.

7) I decree and declare that no previous affliction is permitted to come upon me again, IJN.

8) I command every network between wicked humans and demons opposed to my breakthrough or fortune restoration to scatter by divine fire, IJN.

9) Lord, help me to henceforth never look back at my previous disappointments and losses, and give me the power to move forward to realize the better plans you have for me, IJN.

10) I command all the forces of spiritual instability in my life to scatter by the superior power in the Blood of redemption, IJN.

Additional Prayers for Diverse Purposes and Needs

Q. **Pressing on towards the Mark of the High Calling of God in Christ** *(Philippians 3:12-16; Colossians 1:9-10; Jeremiah 29:11)*

1) Lord, help me to grow steadily in the grace of pleasing you, bearing fruit in every good work, IJN.

2) Lord, help me and my family to grow in the knowledge of God and in our passion for the affairs of your kingdom, IJN.

3) Lord, help me to henceforth run the Christian race with a strong heavenly-minded determination, IJN.

4) Like the Apostle Paul, I resolve to forget the things that lie behind and to shun every worldly distraction as I run the race of eternal life, IJN.

5) Like Paul the Apostle, I resolve to press on to win the prize of the upward call of God in Christ, IJN.

6) Lord, fill me with all the grace to press on towards the mark of the high calling of God in Christ, IJN.

7) Lord, empower me to henceforth live a life worthy of your calling and consecration, IJN.

R. **Commanding the Release of Souls and Riches Held in Spiritual Captivity:** *Corporate and Personal Prayers* *(Isaiah 45:1-4; 54:14-15; Haggai 2:6-7; Luke 4:17-19)*

1) By our corporate anointing, we demand the release of all the recaptured souls that the church has previously laboured to save in our community, IJN.

2) We interrupt the powers of the second heaven, the powers of the first heaven, the powers of the sea, and we set free all the arrested captives that belong to Zion, IJN.

3) We summon the souls of all the remnants of Zion held in captivity to jump out of the habitations of wickedness, IJN.

4) My heavenly Father, by your divine power, I break every invisible curse or chain that hinders my spiritual growth and wholeness, IJN.

5) Lord, may you baptize me with the spirit of boldness for soul-winning, IJN.

6) Lord, kindle in me the passion and fire to go after perishing souls, IJN.

7) Lord, help me to abide strongly in you as a true branch, that I might bear much fruit, IJN.

8) I command all wicked accusations and yokes of darkness upon my life to scatter by fire, IJN.

9) By the mercies in the Blood of Jesus, I command an end to the forces of waste and calamity working against my life and household, IJN.

10) My heavenly Father, may you give your church in our community the treasures hidden in darkness and riches hidden in secret places, IJN.

S. **Commanding Favour in Marital Destiny and Aspirations**
(Genesis 2:18, RSV; Genesis 29:21-31; 41: 39-45; Esther 2:15-18; Proverbs 18:22)

1) By the power in the name of Jesus Christ, I dismantle every spiritual obstacle and stumbling block against my marital destiny, IJN.

2) By the authority of the Living God, I command the deliverance of my marital destiny from all evil covenants and curses of the wicked, IJN.

3) I break every demonic covenant hindering my marital breakthrough and favour, IJN.

4) By the power in the Blood of redemption, I divorce every spiritual spouse blocking or resisting my marital aspirations and destiny, IJN.

5) By the authority in the name of Jesus, I summon the fire of the Lord to consume every spiritual spouse contending against my marriage and marital destiny, IJN.

6) Lord, may you deliver me from marrying the wrong person by error, by an act of desperation, or by a stubborn will, IJN.

7) I break every demonic veil assigned to twist my choice of a marriage partner, IJN.

8) My heavenly Father, may you give me the grace to overcome all my previous setbacks, disappointments and betrayals in relationships, IJN.

Additional Prayers for Diverse Purposes and Needs

9) By the power in the Blood of redemption, I denounce every negative faith I have developed through marital failure and frustration, IJN.

10) According to *Proverbs 18:22*, I believe and confess the Word of the Lord that marriage is a good thing and a source of favour from the Lord, IJN.

11) Lord, help me to build my marriage and home by the wisdom of the Holy Scriptures, IJN.

12) Lord, help me to henceforth commit myself to gaining the necessary spiritual knowledge and wisdom to build my marriage and home on a godly foundation, IJN.

13) I decree and confess that my marriage shall be blessed and full of divine favour, IJN.

14) Lord, release grace upon every marriage and home in our church; may your peace and grace reign in our homes, IJN.

T. **Prayers for the Government and the Governed:** *Personal and Corporate Prayers*
(1 Timothy 2:1-5; Proverbs 29:2 & 16; Romans 13:1-7)

1) Lord, help those in all levels of government in our country to govern with wisdom, the fear of God, and a good conscience, IJN.

2) My heavenly Father, may you frustrate all the counsel of the wicked in positions of political power intended to disadvantage the body of Christ and our land, IJN.

3) By the power in the Blood of redemption, we frustrate all agendas of the wicked to rise to positions of power and influence in the government of this land, IJN.

4) Lord, help our government to make good laws that will increase and expand wealth and prosperity in the land, IJN.

5) Lord, help those in government to govern well, as God's servants for the good of the people, IJN.

6) Lord, give me the grace not to be a law-breaker but to be a law-abiding citizen, IJN.

7) We decree as a church that all our workplaces and residential neighbourhoods shall be crime-free, IJN.

8) Lord, strengthen the law enforcement agents in their work of fighting crime in our neighbourhoods and community, IJN.

9) Lord, may you touch the hearts of hardened criminals in our community and let them encounter your saving grace, IJN.

10) Lord, help your church go with grace and compassion after the souls of hardened criminals and vicious offenders, IJN.

11) Lord, use your church in this land to rescue and rehabilitate many criminal offenders that social services and other secular agencies cannot rehabilitate, IJN.

U. **Restoration of Lost Time and Wasted Years**
(Joel 2:24-27; Ephesians 1:3-4)

1) Lord, forgive me for having in any way mismanaged or wasted my years and productive time, IJN.

2) Lord, pour forth your fire of spiritual revival and divine encounters upon my life and upon the body of Christ in our community, IJN.

3) Lord, release upon me the anointing and grace to overcome the wicked powers fighting against my spiritual growth, IJN.

4) My heavenly Father, by your eternal power, restore to me the years which the devourers have eaten, IJN.

5) Lord, by your sovereign will, restore to me the destiny milestones that I have lost in life due to my own fault, IJN.

6) Lord, by your eternal power, restore to me all recoverable opportunities the enemy has wasted in my life, IJN.

7) By the power in the Blood of redemption, I command an end to the war of desolation and delay launched by the enemy to block my expected miracles, IJN.

8) Lord, raise a victorious voice for me in every place where my case comes under consideration, IJN.

9) By the power of the Lord's restoration, I declare that my reproach and warfare are over, and I shall never again be put to shame, IJN.

10) By the power of the Lord's restoration, I declare that I shall henceforth have all good things in plenty and be satisfied and also have an abundance for every good work, IJN.

Additional Prayers for Diverse Purposes and Needs

V. **Overcoming Every Satanic Siege and Diabolical Pursuer**
(Exodus 14:10-31; 2 Kings 6:8-18; 2 Chronicles 20:17-18; Psalm 35:1-8; Jeremiah 52: 4-11; 2 Thessalonians 1:5-6)

1) Lord, set me free from the grip of besetting sins and help me to conscientiously live above all intentional sins, IJN.

2) By the power in the Blood of redemption, I terminate every demonic siege around my life and household, IJN.

3) By the power in the Blood of redemption, we terminate every demonic siege against our local church, IJN.

4) My heavenly Father, help me to keep my peace while you fight my deliverance battles, IJN.

5) I command every humanly impossible obstacle standing between me and my Promised Land like the Red Sea to be lifted by fire, IJN.

6) I command every yoke of Babylonian siege hanging over my life and household to break by fire, IJN.

7) I decree and declare that I will never serve any wicked task master again in my life, IJN.

8) I command all diabolical pursuers after my life and family to be drowned by the vengeance of the Living God, IJN.

9) I refuse to be dismayed because the Lord is with me in every battle of life, IJN.

10) I command every messenger of darkness assigned to take me or any member of my family into captivity to be disarmed and vanquished, IJN.

11) I destroy every arrest warrant issued against me in the regions of darkness, IJN.

12) I break and scatter every alliance and conspiracy of the wicked against my advancement in life, IJN.

13) Lord, give me the grace to face every opposition of the enemy and to prevail over it, IJN.

14) Let the wrath of the Lord terrify all the wicked enchanters casting spells of misfortune against me and my family, IJN.

15) Lord, cause the fear of me to overwhelm the thoughts of all my wicked adversaries, IJN.

16) Lord, assign your warring angels to mount a counter-siege to overpower and defeat all our stubborn adversaries, IJN.

17) Lord, unleash terrifying disasters against all those blocking my divine opportunities and progress in this land, IJN.

18) My heavenly Father, manifest your victory and glory in all areas of my life, IJN.

W. **Defeating All Those Who Attack Me without a Cause**
(Psalm 55:1-3; 9-19; Isaiah 7:1-7; Isaiah 8:9-10)

1) I nullify every evil counsel and decree released by the wicked against me and my household, IJN.

2) I decree that no contrary counsel or judgement issued against me or my household shall stand, IJN.

3) I command every counsel the Lord has not commanded against me and my family to scatter by fire, IJN.

4) I overrule and nullify all decrees which the Lord has not commanded against our local church, IJN.

5) I command every midnight terror and oppression of the wicked against me and my loved ones to scatter, IJN.

6) I command all witchcraft voices of the wicked against me and my family to be wasted by fire, IJN.

7) By the power in the Blood of redemption, I terminate all the evil devices of witchcraft hurting me and my family, IJN.

8) By divine authority, I command all the violent devices and terror of the wicked against our land to be destroyed, IJN.

9) By the power in the Blood of redemption, I break every implant of ancestral curse and infirmity running through my bloodline, IJN.

10) My heavenly Father, may you heal, sanctify and wash me afresh in the precious Blood of redemption, IJN.

11) Lord, overshadow me and my household with your manifold power and favour, IJN.

Additional Prayers for Diverse Purposes and Needs

X. **Faithfulness in Unrighteous Mammon and Working for True Riches** *(Deuteronomy 8:18; Proverbs 15:16; Luke 16:9-13; John 4:33-38, 1 Chronicles 4:10)*

1) Lord, deliver me and my family from the curse of unrighteous wages, IJN.

2) I dismantle by fire all the satanic authorities monitoring my life, progress and finances, IJN.

3) I belong to the Lord Jesus and to Him alone; therefore, I refuse to serve any mammon spirit, IJN.

4) Every curse in my life and family rooted in the love of money, be nullified by the power in the Blood of redemption, IJN.

5) By the power in the Blood of redemption, I break every curse of unrighteous mammon and unjust revenue operating in my life and household, IJN.

6) Lord, give me the grace to be faithful to you with money; to be faithful in giving God His due in all my earnings, IJN.

7) Lord Jesus, give me the grace to be reckoned among the faithful stewards you can trust with money, IJN.

8) By the power in the name of Jesus, I break every control that mammon spirits have over my life, IJN.

9) I bind and cast out all arrows of failure fired into my finances and destiny, IJN.

10) I proclaim and declare that the Lord is my helper, I shall not fear; there is nothing that the wicked can do to me, IJN.

11) I bind and cast out every arrow of infirmity fired into my body, IJN.

12) By the power in the Blood of redemption, I break every evil yoke upon my health and destiny, IJN.

13) I command every inherited pattern of generational poverty operating in my life to be broken, IJN.

14) I command all wicked spirits enforcing financial lack and closed doors in my life to scatter, IJN.

15) My heavenly Father, help me to prioritize spreading the good news of salvation to win souls for eternal life, IJN.

16) My heavenly Father, may you give me the wisdom and power to get and manage wealth, IJN.

17) Lord, give me the grace to only work for true riches through the fear of God, IJN.

18) By the power in the name of Jesus, I command resources and opportunities to flow from my heavenly account to my earthly account, IJN.

19) My heavenly Father, let my heavenly treasures henceforth speak territorial enlargement, both spiritual and material, upon my life (according to *1 Chronicles 4:10*), IJN.

Y. **Overcoming the Wickedness of the Wicked:** *Personal and Corporate Prayers* (*Psalm 7:9; Proverbs 4:16-17, AMP; Exodus 22:18, RSV; Nehemiah 2:9:10; 19-20, RSV; Hebrew 6:7-8, RSV*)

1) Lord Jesus, I thank you for the joy of this day and for the open heaven you have set before us, IJN.

2) Lord, show mercy to us, our country and our government, IJN.

3) Lord, by your divine power, we command the wickedness of the wicked to come to an end in our local church, IJN.

4) Lord, by your divine power, I command the wickedness of the wicked to come to an end in my life and family, IJN.

5) By the power in the Blood of redemption, I decree and declare that the wicked are not permitted to block my open heaven, IJN.

6) Lord, may you expand your kingdom and the reign of righteousness in our land through the preaching of your gospel, IJN.

7) My heavenly Father, may you increase in me the grace to bear good fruit that befit repentance, IJN.

8) Lord, give me the grace to cut off evil doers from my life, IJN.

9) My heavenly Father, may you disappoint the negative imaginations of all those who are displeased that you have remembered and favoured me, IJN.

10) I command every false accusation and ganging-up of the wicked against me and my family to scatter by fire, IJN.

11) By the power in the Blood of redemption, I command every wicked agent of Satan assigned to waste my life and destiny to be wasted, IJN.

12) By the power in the Blood of redemption, we shield the lives and destinies of all the children in our local church from the destructive enterprises of the wicked, IJN.

13) I proclaim and declare that neither I nor my household will be casualties of wickedness by witchcraft, IJN.

14) My heavenly Father, may you deploy your warring angels to fight and win all my battles, IJN.

15) By the creative power in the Spirit of redemption, I reverse every damage the wicked have done in my life and in the lives of my household members, IJN.

16) Thank you, Lord, for all the answers to our prayers, IJN.

Z. **Reaffirming God's Faithfulness to His Word, Promises and Covenant** *(Luke 1:45, KJV)*

1) Lord, I thank you for your faithfulness to your inspired words, promises, dreams, visions and prophecies, IJN.

2) Lord, help me to be faithful to you in all things from today, moving forward, IJN.

3) By the authority in the name of Jesus, I believe and declare that there shall be a performance of those things which were spoken to me from the Lord, IJN.

4) Lord, help me to be consistent in my faith and confession, that there shall be a performance of these things spoken to me from the Lord, IJN.

5) Lord, give me the grace to wait in patience and prayerful expectation for a performance of the promises of the Lord in my life and household, IJN.

6) I scatter by fire every contrary altar contending against the performance of God's promises for the church of Jesus Christ in our community, IJN.

7) I dismantle by fire every contrary altar contending against the performance of God's promises to me and my household, IJN.

8) I shall not die but live in peace and good health, to take full possession of all the blessings spoken to me from the Lord, IJN.

9) By the power in the Blood of redemption, I claim the covenant blessings of Abraham upon my life—blessings of good health, protection, productivity, longevity, riches and all-round favours, IJN.

10) Lord, thank you for over-answering all my prayers, IJN.

Endnotes

[1] The empirical evidence for this observation could be found by looking at some of the countries in the bottom quartile of the World Happiness Index, Human Development Index, and Fragile States Index, over the preceding 5 years. In the list are many highly prayerful countries with large Christian populations (especially countries in Africa, with just a few turbulent countries in Latin America and the Middle East).

[2] See, Adoyo (2006:1212). Bonifes E. Adoyo is a retired bishop of the Kenyan-based *Christ Is The Answer Ministries* (CITAM) and former head of the *Evangelical Alliance of Kenya*. He is a respected Bible teacher.

[3] Kenneth E. Hagin, "Why Pray?", https://www.cfaith.com/index.php/blog/24-articles/prayer/18165-why-pray

[4] Kenneth E. Hagin, Ibid.

[5] Paraphrased from *Philippians 2:5-11, NLT,* and *John 14:10-11.*

[6] Paraphrased from *Acts 4:10-12*; *Matthew 17:5*; and *John 14:12-14.*

[7] This is the definition of prevailing prayer by Wesley Duewel in his book, *Mighty Prevailing Prayer* (1990), quoted and illustrated by H. O. Nzeakor (2008) in *Power Through Morning Prayer: Divine Breakfast*, Nsukka: Revival Publications, p.26

[8] Charles G. Finney (n.d.) "Prevailing Prayer", https://www.path2prayer.com/revival-and-the-holy-spirit/charles-finney/charles-finney-prevailing-prayer

[9] Charles Finney (n.d.) *Memoirs*, pp. 363-365, https://www.path2prayer.com/revival-and-the-holy-spirit/charles-finney/the-means-used-in-charles-finneys-revivals

[10] Charles G. Finney, (n.d.) "Prevailing Prayer", https://www.path2prayer.com/revival-and-the-holy-spirit/charles-finney/charles-finney-prevailing-prayer

[11] See the parallel Bible commentaries on *James 5:16 (KJV)*; specifically, *Benson Commentary, Barnes' Notes on the Bible*, and *Gill's Exposition of the Entire Bible*, at https://Biblehub.com/commentaries/james/5-16.htm#

[12] In this sentence, my description of the symptoms of AKN that I experienced have been adapted from an article published in a professional website on the disease by Kathryn Khadija Leverette (2018) "Acne Keloidalis, Scalp Bumps and Scars": https://clinicallyclear.com/acne-keloidalis

[13] Marriage is in line with God's will for humanity: *Proverbs 18:22* says, "He who finds a wife finds a good thing and obtains favour from the Lord." I have discussed the issue of marriage as part of God's will, in a different book I published in 2015 titled *Preparing for Marriage and Enjoying Marriage*. It suffices to say that all the promises of the scriptures and God's miracles can be received if one has a believing knowledge of the truth and prays in faith.

[14] There has been a longstanding theological debate about the translation of the first part of *Matthew 6:13*: "And lead us not into temptation." Most Christian theologians claim that this is a mistranslation applicable to the English Bible. Proponents argue that God does not lead us into temptation because the Bible is not self-contradictory; as it is written in *James 1:13-15*: "Let no one say when he is tempted, 'I am tempted by God'; for God cannot be tempted by evil, nor does He Himself tempt anyone. But each one is tempted when he is drawn away by his own desires and enticed. Then, when desire has conceived, it gives birth to sin; and sin, when it is full-grown, brings forth death." Taking sides with proponents of a flawed translation in the English Bible, the Catholic Pontiff Pope Francis in December 2017 revealed that "he wanted to amend the line 'lead us not into temptation'". The New Testament Bible was

originally written in Greek, while the Old Testament was largely written in Hebrew, with a small part in Aramaic. On 22 May 2019, Pope Francis approved the changing of those supposedly mistranslated words of Our Lord's Prayer for the Catholic Church to "do not let us fall into temptation". For details of this story, see *Sky News* (6/06/2019), "Pope Francis Approves Changes to Words of Lord's Prayer", https://news.sky.com/story/pope-francis-approves-changes-to-words-of-lords-prayer-11736368

[15] The old King James Bible (KJV) uses the phrase "speaking in an unknown tongue" (*1 Corinthians 14:2*) to describe praying in the spirit, a qualifier that most modern Bible translations, including the NKJV, avoid. The tongue or language in which one prays in the spirit is clearly known to God and could sometimes be known to men, as the example of the first Holy Spirit baptism in *Acts 2:1-13* demonstrates. The disciples who received the baptism of the Holy Spirit were all Galileans who spoke in diverse languages that the inhabitants and visitors in Jerusalem from different nationalities understood to be their respective languages.

[16] In the Bible, the mantle symbolizes God's authority, anointing and enabling power given to individuals. The mantle can also represent the anointing of the Holy Spirit for a specific calling.

[17] Taken from the sermon by Bishop David Oyedepo titled, "Winning the War of Life," posted online on 19 December 2020. Words in italics are my emphasis. https://www.youtube.com/watch?v=DtvnObDkKWY&t=9s

[18] There are diverse structural explanations for extreme poverty and high infant mortality rates in many developing countries; not least, the disadvantages that these countries suffer in the global system of trade, often compounded by the problem of bad governance.

[19] See Andrews (2021: xx-xxvii). Kehinde Andrews is a British professor of Black Studies at Birmingham City University, UK.

[20] See Truelove (2020). Sam Truelove is Content Editor for *My London*, part of Reach plc, Britain's largest newspaper, magazine and digital publisher with a print and online portfolio.

[21] Adapted *mutatis mutandis* from Kenneth E. Hagin (1993:23).

[22] See Hagin (1993:22).

[23] This definition is adapted from *Hebrews 11:1* and is partly enriched by my own illustration and the paper by Carrie Lowrance, "What Is Faith and Why Is It Important?" *Crosswalk.com*, 5 January 2022, https://www.crosswalk.com/faith/spiritual-life/what-is-faith-definition-importance.html

[24] Lester Sumrall (1913–1996) was a great American missionary, miracle worker and faith preacher. The entire quote is an extract from a sermon he preached, titled "Dr Lester Sumrall—The Greatest Message on Faith Ever Preached!" posted on YouTube on 5 March 2019. All the italicized words are my emphasis. https://www.youtube.com/watch?v=_OlqDRgRqG4

[25] The italicized words are my emphasis.

[26] See Wommack (n.d.).

[27] Hagin (1993:22).

[28] Taken from the sermon by the great American evangelist T. L. Osborn, titled: "How to Make Your Faith Work for You," posted on YouTube on 11 November 2022, https://www.youtube.com/watch?v=fWhuOKbounU

[29] See Oppenheimer (2015).

[30] See Goeke (2016) and Lynch (2023).

[31] See Fritz Chery (2023), "Bible Verses About Storms" 17 May, https://Biblereasons.com/storms/. The italicized words are my emphasis.

[32] The "lawful captives" refer to all those that the devil has a spiritual legal ground to capture and afflict because of their trespasses or disobedience to God or for other reasons.

Bibliography

Adayo, E. Bonifes (2006). "Prayer" in Tokumbo Adeyemo (ed.) *Africa Bible Commentary*. Nairobi: WordAlive Publishers, p.1212 (a one-page article).

Andrews, Kehinde (2021). *The New Age of Empire: How Racism and Colonialism Still Rule the World*. London: Allen Lane.

Baros, John (2019). "The Power of Prevailing Prayers," *The Apostolic Faith Magazine*, 15 Sep, https://www.apostolicfaith.org/the-apostolic-faith/the-power-of-prevailing-prayer

Fairchild, Mary (2021). "How Does the Bible Define Faith?" *Learn Religions*, 6 January, https://www.learnreligions.com/what-is-the-meaning-of-faith-700722

Goeke, Niklas (2016). "The Power of Positive Thinking Summary," *Four Minutes Books*, 9 April. https://fourminutebooks.com/the-power-of-positive-thinking-summary/

Hagin, E. Kenneth (1991). *The Interceding Christian*. Tulsa OK: RHEMA Bible Church.

Hagin, E. Kenneth (1993). *The Triumphant Church: Dominion Over All the Powers of Darkness*. Tulsa OK: RHEMA Bible Church.

Hagin, E. Kenneth (2007). *The Art of Prayer: A Handbook on How to Pray*. (Fourth ed.) Tulsa OK: RHEMA Bible Church.

Hagin, E. Kenneth (2017). "Faith Is a Spiritual Force," *Word of Faith Magazine*, June/July. https://www.rhema.org/index.php?option=com_content&view=article&id=2663:faith-is-a-spiritual-force&catid=266&Itemid=11 (Kenneth Hagin Ministries)

Kegan, Patrick (2021). *Bouncing Forwards: Notes on Resilience, Courage and Change*. Surrey: Waverley Abbey Resources.

Lynch, Mark (2023). "20 All-Time Best Motivational Books to Inspire You," *LifeHack*, 9 March. https://www.lifehack.org/842960/motivational-books

Meyer, Joyce (1995). *Battlefield of the Mind: Winning the Battle in the Mind*. New York: Warner Faith Publishers.

Oliver, Robert (2019). "Conditional Blessings of God," *The Sampson Independent*, 6 Sep. https://www.clintonnc.com/news/religion/42247/conditional-blessings-of-god#:~:text=Some%20of%20God's%20promises%20are,9%3A11

Omartian, Stormie (2005). *The Power of a Praying Teen*. Oregon: Harvest House Publishers.

Oppenheimer, Mark (2015). "An Illustrated Guide to the 613 Jewish Commandments," *The New York Times*, 30 Oct, https://www.nytimes.com/2015/10/31/us/an-illustrated-guide-to-the-613-jewish-commandments.html#:~:text=But%20there%20are%20more%3A%20From,of%20the%20613%20are%20obsolete

Prince, Derek (2009). *Secrets of a Prayer Warrior*. Grand Rapids, MI: Derek Prince Ministries Intl.

Ramirez, John (2021). *Conquer Your Deliverance: How to Live a Life of Total Freedom*. Minneapolis: Chosen Publishers.

Truelove, Sam (2020). "London's Most Fearsome Gang, Their Nicknames and How They Became Notorious on Streets," *My London*, 13 Nov. https://www.mylondon.news/news/nostalgia/most-fearsome-gang-nicknames-how-19277916

Wilkinson, Bruce (2000). *The Prayer of Jabez: Breaking Through to the Blessed Life*. Sisters, Oregon: Multnomah Publishers.

Wommack, Andrew (n.d.) "Faith Is Based on Knowledge," Andrew Wommack Ministries, https://www.awmi.net/reading/teaching-articles/faith_knowledge/#:~:text=So%20faith%20must%20come%20through,difficult%20to%20operate%20in%20faith.

Index

A
Abel, *129*
Abraham, *23, 63, 85, 87, 90, 93, 96, 98, 103, 114, 124-126, 130-131*
Acne Keloidalis Nuchae, *39*
Adam, *vii, viii, 14-15, 17, 96*
Adoyo, Bonifes, *14*
Ahab, King, *18, 63, 86-87, 97-98*
Ahaziah, King, *86, 98*
AKN, *39-41*, *See* Acne Keloidalis Nuchae

B
Bad fight of the flesh, the, *83*
Baptism of the Holy Spirit, *See* Holy Spirit, baptism of the
Baros, John, *23*
Born again, *ix, x, 21, 26-27, 35, 40, 41, 47, 66, 68, 69, 119, 124*

C
Caleb, *123*
Community background, *89-92*
Cornelius, *27*
Covenant blessings, *131*
Critical Race Theory, *89*

D
Daniel, *57, 132*
David, King, *45, 70, 76, 77, 87, 94, 96, 133*
Deliverance, *20, 21, 39, 47, 51-52, 85, 102*
Demons, *vii, 17, 30, 41-42, 52, 53, 74, 116, 119*
  demonic attacks, *51*
  demonic oppression, *52*
  demonization, *42*
  demon-possession, *41*
Destiny, *24, 57, 81, 93-96, 101-102*
Devil, *14, 15, 21, 31, 32, 39, 42, 46, 47, 51, 57, 82-83, 90, 91, 93-96, 100, 104, 105, 115, 117, 131, See* Satan
Dominion mandate, *vii, viii, 14-18*

E
Elijah, *vi, 18, 35-36, 125*
Enoch, *130*
Eve, *vii, viii, 14-15, 17, 96, See* Adam
Ezekiel, *87, 88*

F
Fairchild, Mary, *104*
Faith
  counterfeit, *119*
  genuine, *23, 119*
  good fight of, *81-83, 133*
  measures of, *114, 119-121, 127*
  personal, *v, 14, 104-107, 109, 111, 113-117, 129-133*
  levels of, *113-115*
Faith declaration(s), *17, 20*
Faith without works, *30, 110*
Familiar spirits, *28, 32*
Fasting, *45-48, 52, 57, 63, 65, 66, 69, 70, 72, 82*
Finney, Charles, *19-20, 35*

H
Habakkuk, *106*
Hagin, Kenneth E., *14, 47, 62, 91, 106, 127*
Healing, *20, 21, 39, 41, 49, 51-54, 102, 105, 108-109, 115, 116, 125, 126*
Holy Spirit, *vii, x, 14, 21, 22, 25, 30, 33, 35-36, 42, 43, 48, 50, 58, 61, 62, 66- 69, 77, 82, 100, 102, 109, 122, 124*
  baptism of the, *x, 67-69, 115*
  gifts of the, *48, 49, 109*
  indwelling, *16, 21, 41, 49, 72, 100, 104*
  partnership with the, *14, 18, 50, 107, 122*

I
Institutional racism, *89*
Intercessory prayer, *66*
Isaac, *93, 98, 126, 130-131, See* Abraham

J
Jabez, *64-65*
  prayer of, *64*
Jacob, *22, 23, 24, 93, 98, 126, 131*
James, Apostle, *36, 53*
Jehoshaphat, *86, 97, 98*
Jeremiah, *31, 32, 57, 94*
Jesus Christ, *vii, viii, ix, x, 15-18, 36, 41, 46, 47, 50, 51, 66, 68, 71, 74, 75, 81, 82, 95, 108, 109, 125*
John, Apostle, *33*
John the Baptist, *61, 82, 93, 125, 126*
Joseph, *57, 93, 94, 96*
Joshua, *98*

Index

K
King, Martin Luther, Jr., *91*
Kingdom of darkness, *vii, viii, x, 16, 37, 39, 46, 47, 74, 82, 84, 89, 131*
Kingdom of God, *ix, x, 39, 48, 49, 54, 56, 81, 111*

L
Logos, *106, 107, 111, 120, See* Rhema
Lying prophecy, *31*

M
Measures of faith, *114, 119-121, 127*
  great faith, *125*
  little faith, *106, 114, 120, 121, 123-124*
  small faith, *123-124*
  strong faith, *114, 124*
  violent faith, *126*
Meyer, Joyce, *22*
Midnight prayers, *39-41, 68*
Ministry of prayer, *18*
Miracle(s), *15, 18, 20, 21, 28, 39, 52, 64, 71, 75, 102, 105, 107, 108, 109, 110, 114, 120, 122, 124, 125, 127*
Moses, *76, 93, 112, 123, 132*

N
Naaman, *110*
Nebuchadnezzar, *57, 72, 76*
Nehemiah, *77, 160*
Noah, *103, 130*

O
Oliver, Robert, *112*
Omartian, Stormie, *77*
Osborn, T.L., *110*
Our Lord's Prayer, *3, 17, 61, 63*
Oyedepo, David (Bishop), *81*

P
Paul, Apostle, *28, 38-40, 51, 56-58, 65, 68, 69, 81, 83, 90, 99, 110, 114, 119*
Peale, Norman Vincent, *122*
Peter, Apostle, *87, 90, 117*
Prayer
  corporate, *74-75*
  of inquiry, *70*
  power of, *v, 14, 25*
  prevailing, *viii, 19, 20, 22-25*
Prayers
  of authority, *71*
  prevailing, *vii, viii, 20-21, 35, 105*
Praying
  in the spirit, *67-69*
  in tongues, *63, 69*
Prince, Derek, *34-35*

R
Rahab, *133*
Ramirez, John, *84-85*
Repentance of the righteous, *47*
Rhema, *57-58, 106-107, 111, 120*

S
Samson, *93, 94, 96, 133*
Sanctification, *49*
Sarah, *87, 93, 96, 114, 124, 130, See* Abraham
Satan, *vii-viii, x, 14-17, 28, 37, 40, 47, 63, 71, 74, 82, 84, 85, 93, 94, 114, 117, 121*
  satanic altars, *84*
  satanic bondage, *84*
  satanic deception, *46-47, 119*
  satanic warlock, *84*
  satanic kingdom, *viii, x, See* Kingdom of darkness
Saul, *70, 76, 94*
Self-edification, *67, 69*
Social identity, *89-90, 92*
Sorcerers, *28, 42-43, See* Familiar spirits
Soul-winning, *46, 50, 116*
Spirit of divination, *28, 32*
Spiritual healing contest, *108*
Spiritual warfare, *18, 21, 72*
Spiritual attacks, *48*
Spiritual battle, *41, 48, 124*
Strongholds, *18, 71, 92*
Sumrall, Lester, *103*

T
Thanksgiving, *17, 37-39, 64, 67, 77*
Timothy, *57, 58, 65, 81, 83, 119*

W
Wesley, John, *16*
Wilkinson, Bruce, *64*
Will of God, *viii, 16-19, 25, 34-36, 44-46, 48-50, 55, 58, 59, 61, 64, 67, 70, 72, 75, 95*
Witches, *42-43, 115*
  witchcraft attacks, *43*
Wommack, Andrew, *104*

About the Author

Kenneth Omeje is, by the mercies of God, a minister of the gospel, Bible teacher, academic researcher, and prolific author. Since December 2013, he has served as the Presiding Pastor of Crown of Christ Gospel Church in Bradford, United Kingdom. He received part of his ministerial training at The Emancipation Ministries (TEM) in Nigeria, where he also served as an ordained Deacon and Locum Minister in the 1990s. He later joined the Wesley Reformed Church in West Yorkshire, UK, for four years and, subsequently, the Redeemed Christian Church of God (RCCG), where he served as the pioneer pastor of RCCG Chapel of Grace in Shipley, UK, from June 2007 to December 2008.

Kenneth holds a PhD degree in Peace Studies from the University of Bradford and has over thirty years of professional experience as an academic in various universities in Africa, Europe and North America. He has authored several publications that cut across the social sciences, religion in Africa, and the Christian faith. His previous Christian books include *Understanding Divine Destiny* (2015) and *Preparing for Marriage and Enjoying Marriage* (2015). Kenneth teaches and preaches the gospel of Jesus Christ with manifold grace and true apostolic miracles.

Printed in Dunstable, United Kingdom